The Last Road North

A GUIDE TO THE GETTYSBURG CAMPAIGN, 1863

by Robert Orrison and Dan Welch

EMERGING CIVIL WAR SERIES

Chris Mackowski, series editor
Kristopher D. White, chief historian

Also part of the Emerging Civil War Series

The Aftermath of Battle: The Burial of the Civil War Dead
   by Meg Groeling

Bloody Autumn: The Shenandoah Valley Campaign of 1864
   by Daniel T. Davis and Phillip S. Greenwalt

Bushwhacking on a Grand Scale: The Battle of Chickamauga, September 18-20, 1863
   by William Lee White

Calamity in Carolina: The Battles of Averasboro and Bentonville, March 1865
   by Daniel T. Davis and Phillip S. Greenwalt

Dawn of Victory: Breakthrough at Petersburg, March 25-April 2, 1865
   by Edward S. Alexander

Fight Like the Devil: The First Day at Gettysburg, July 1, 1863
   by Chris Mackowski, Kristopher D. White, and Daniel T. Davis

Grant's Last Battle: The Story Behind the Personal Memoirs of Ulysses S. Grant
   by Chris Mackowski

Hell Itself: The Battle of the Wilderness, May 5-7, 1864
   by Chris Mackowski

Hurricane from the Heavens: The Battle of Cold Harbor, May 26-June 5, 1864
   by Daniel T. Davis and Phillip S. Greenwalt

The Last Days of Stonewall Jackson: The Mortal Wounding of the Confederacy's Greatest Icon
   by Chris Mackowski and Kristopher D. White

No Turning Back: A Guide to the 1864 Overland Campaign
   by Robert M. Dunkerly, Donald C. Pfanz, and David R. Ruth

Out Flew the Sabres: The Battle of Brandy Station, June 9, 1863
   by Eric J. Wittenberg and Daniel T. Davis

A Season of Slaughter: The Battle of Spotsylvania Court House, May 8-21, 1864
   by Chris Mackowski and Kristopher D. White

Simply Murder: The Battle of Fredericksburg, December 13, 1862
   by Chris Mackowski and Kristopher D. White

Strike Them a Blow: Battle Along the North Anna River, May 21-25, 1864
   by Chris Mackowski

That Furious Struggle: Chancellorsville and the High Tide of the Confederacy, May 1-4, 1863
   by Chris Mackowski and Kristopher D. White

To the Bitter End: Appomattox, Bennett Place, and the Surrenders of the Confederacy
   by Robert M. Dunkerly

A Want of Vigilance: The Bristoe Station Campaign, October 9-19, 1863
   by Bill Backus and Rob Orrison

The Last Road North

A GUIDE TO THE GETTYSBURG CAMPAIGN, 1863

by Robert Orrison and Dan Welch

EMERGING CIVIL WAR SERIES

SB
Savas Beatie
California

First edition, first printing

ISBN (paperback): 978-1-61121-243-3
ISBN (ebook): 978-1-61121-244-0

Library of Congress Cataloging-in-Publication Data

Names: Welch, Dan, (Educator), author. | Orrison, Robert, author.
Title: The last road north : a guide to the Gettysburg Campaign, 1863 / by
Dan Welch and Robert Orrison.
Description: First edition. | El Dorado Hills, California : Savas Beatie,
2016. | Series: Emerging Civil War series
Identifiers: LCCN 2016014360| ISBN 9781611212433 (pbk) | ISBN
9781611212440
(ebk)
Subjects: LCSH: Gettysburg Campaign, 1863--Guidebooks. | United
States--History--Civil War, 1861-1865--Campaigns--Guidebooks.
Classification: LCC E475.51 .W45 2016 | DDC 973.7/349--dc23
LC record available at https://lccn.loc.gov/2016014360

SB

Published by
Savas Beatie LLC
989 Governor Drive, Suite 102
El Dorado Hills, California 95762
Phone: 916-941-6896
Email: sales@savasbeatie.com
Web: www.savasbeatie.com

Savas Beatie titles are available at special discounts for bulk purchases in the United
States by corporations, institutions, and other organizations. For more details, please
contact Special Sales, P.O. Box 4527, El Dorado Hills, CA 95762, or you may e-mail
us as at sales@savasbeatie.com, or visit our website at www.savasbeatie.com for
additional information.

Dedicated to the thousands of men, North and South, whose march to Gettysburg was their "last road north."

Table of Contents

Brandy Station served as the opening engagement of the Gettysburg campaign. Fleetwood Hill stands as the battlefield's most prominent landmark. (dw)

List of Maps

Maps by Hal Jespersen

Footnotes for this volume are available at http://emergingcivilwar.com/publications/the-emerging-civil-war-series/footnotes

Acknowledgments

We first would like to thank Chris Mackowski (editor-in-chief Emerging Civil War) for being the force behind the Emerging Civil War project. Thank you to Ted Savas and the staff at Savas Beatie for the opportunity to work on this project and promote Civil War scholarship. Hal Jespersen again availed to us his cartography skills, and we believe these maps are some of the best maps available relating to the Gettysburg campaign.

Tackling a topic that has the word "Gettysburg" in it is daunting for any student of history. But we felt that we knew the right people to assist us in telling the story of how the men, both Blue and Gray, got to Gettysburg. The battle did not happen in a vacuum, and the town was not pre-determined as a location for the battle. We attempted to put the battle in context of the events leading up to and after the three days in July. We also realize that each stop we have included could have many more words written about it, as there are many more places one could visit. Working with a hard word count helped us stay focused, but we encourage the reader to explore each location in more detail.

Some individuals we would like to thank personally include Clark "Bud" Hall who has not only been an expert on Brandy Station and the Gettysburg Campaign, but also is the main reason many of these places are preserved. We owe a debt of gratitude to Bud for his assistance with this and many other projects. Mike Block, also an expert on Civil War Culpeper, was kind enough to read portions of the manuscript and make helpful suggestions. Gettysburg cavalry expert Eric Wittenberg also was a sounding board for information and recommendations, especially with Stuart's Ride. Historian Bob O'Neill read over the sections on the Loudoun Valley cavalry battles; we look forward to the re-release of his book on these battles.

Our good friend John Tole of the Rappahannock County Historical Society was essential in following the routes of march through Rappahannock County, Virginia. John spent countless hours taking us down original roads and visiting the many homes and structures that still stand today in Rappahannock County that witnessed the Confederate march in June and July 1863. Historian Sean Chick also read the manuscript using his unique perspective of a professional tour guide. Frederick County tourism guru and Civil War expert John Fieseler added some great content for the Union advance through Frederick County. Brian McEnany provided insight into the Army of the Potomac's movements through northern Virginia and helped clear up "Left Wing vs. Right Wing" of the Army of the Potomac.

Craig Swain, a well-known Civil War blogger and historian, was a big help in following the Army of the Potomac through Virginia and especially at Edwards Ferry along the Potomac River. No one can talk about the Federal army in northern Virginia in June 1863 unless they have consulted Craig. Loudoun County historians Tracy and Rich Gillespie

The Potomac River, seen here at Edward's Ferry, marked a significant political as well as geographic boundary during the Gettysburg campaign. (cs)

shared their knowledge of the cavalry battles in the Loudoun Valley between Stuart and Pleasonton. Both are good friends and have supported many of our projects. Kris White read the entire manuscript and provided excellent guidance; his work with ECW has led to a very successful blog, book series, and annual symposium. "Civil War Traveler" Don Pierce is probably the only person we know that has been to every one of these sites. His insight and expertise on seeing these places from the point of view of the Civil War buff was important in developing the tour. Don has been a great friend to us and everyone who works in the Civil War tourism field.

The one-of-a-kind Matt Atkinson also provided many insights that were helpful to put this project into context of other Gettysburg books. Matt is one of the best interpreters we know and has always been willing to assist when we had questions. John Miller with the Monterey Pass Battlefield is the expert on fighting in and around Monterey Pass as well as Lee's retreat from Gettysburg. John and his partners at the Friends of the Monterey Pass Battlefield, Inc., have single-handedly preserved portions of the battlefield, built a wonderful museum, and told the story of the events around the days after Gettysburg. John spent hours showing us sites along the retreat and assisting us with the manuscript.

It is impossible to list everyone who assisted us with research, gave us advice and support. If we forgot anyone, we are at fault and please know it is not because your support is not appreciated.

DAN: This book would never have been possible without the staff at Gettysburg National Military Park, past and present, who gave a young college kid interested in Civil War history a shot at an internship, and, later, the chance to join the staff as a seasonal Park Ranger in the Interpretation Division. Those generosities and experiences changed my life forever. My thanks to Rob Orrison for agreeing to come onto the project during a time when his expertise was needed most. His knowledge of Civil War Virginia and related sites is second to none, and he continues to inspire me with each visit to the Old Dominion state. I also owe my thanks to the man who started this journey for me, my late father. He led me, at the tender age of five, to Gettysburg on a vacation. It was truly an American rite of passage. His father had done it with his family, and my father felt it was something he needed to pass on. A boy with a kepi, toy musket, and storytelling father saw the events of 1863 on those hallowed fields. It sparked a passion for learning and remembrance to this day. Thank you, Dad. Finally, thanks to my wife for her continual support. Without her patience at bookstores, battlefields, and everywhere in between, I would not be able to enjoy these endeavors that inspire me every day.

ROB: Everyone interested in the Civil War remembers that first visit to Gettysburg, and for me, it is no different. I dragged my parents to Gettysburg many years ago, and those memories of seeing the Angle and Little Round Top for the first time are still with me. I appreciate them every time I wake up and "do history" for a career. Thanks to Dan Welch for including me in this project; any written work about Gettysburg is an intimidating undertaking. We both agreed our goal was to write a book that would put Gettysburg in a larger context of the war and allow readers to actually see and experience the places of history. The armies didn't "just show up" at Gettysburg—a lot of "what ifs" and "maybes" happened along the way. The question I get asked the most by people on tour is "did the armies just show up here and fight or run into each other here by accident?" I hope this book gives some insight into how and why they ended up at this Pennsylvania crossroads town. Finally, thanks to my family for the continual support for a hobby that is more than just a hobby. Without them, I would not be able to work on these projects and follow a childhood dream.

PHOTO CREDITS:
Clark Hall (ch); Chris Mackowski (cm); Craig Swain (cs); Dan Welch (dw); Emerging Civil War (ecw); Fold3.com (f3); Francis Delafield Wright, III (fw); Gettysburg National Military Park (gnmp); *Harpers Weekly* (hw); John Miller (jm); Library of Virginia (lova); Library of Congress (loc); Michael Waricher (mw) National Archives (na); Occoquan Historical Society (ohs); Photographic History of the Civil War (phocw); Richard Gillespie (rg); Rob Orrison (ro); United States Army Military History Institute (usamhi); Walter Clark (wc)

For the Emerging Civil War Series

Theodore P. Savas, *publisher*
Chris Mackowski, *series editor*
Kristopher D. White, *chief historian*
Sarah Keeney, *editorial consultant*

Maps by Hal Jespersen
Design and layout by H.R. Gordon
Publication supervision by Chris Mackowski

Touring the Battlefields

This book covers a wide geographic region, from central Virginia to central Pennsylvania. Since the armies marched in routes far apart from each other, this book is divided into different tour routes: the Confederate Advance, the Union Response, Jeb Stuart's Ride to Gettysburg, and the Retreat from Gettysburg. The first three tours end at Gettysburg National Military Park, though at different locations in the Park. The last chapter on the Retreat from Gettysburg begins at the Seminary Ridge Museum in Gettysburg.

Civil War Trails markers, like the one here at Rose Hill, help visitors understand what they're seeing when they visit a site. (dw)

Many of the sites are part of the popular Civil War Trails program and have accessible interpretive markers. The Civil War Trails guide brochure "Gettysburg Campaign: Invasion and Retreat" is a helpful accessory, as many of the sites in the brochure are part of this book. For more information on Civil War Trails, visit *www.civilwartrails.org*.

Although this guide book will follow the general route of the armies, there are a few side trips and optional stops, so please be sure to consult the written directions to each stop. GPS coordinates are also provided for each stop. This book serves as a general guide for sites in the Gettysburg campaign. We have no illusions to cover every site and route used in June-July 1863, but we think this book will introduce people to some sites of which they are unaware.

Be aware that the routes to Gettysburg are each approximately 120 miles and that the retreat route is approximately 50 miles. At a few locations, the tour routes may intersect each other, but the majority of the routes are far apart and cannot be done congruently. Many of the locations can also be further investigated at individual battlefield sites or museums, often both. Take your time and enjoy all that these locations have to offer. We encourage you to support their work in preservation.

In some instances, this tour will pass properties that are privately owned. Please do not trespass.

As much as possible, the tour routes will follow the actual roads that the armies took in 1863. Keep in mind that some roads are rural routes, and others may have heavy traffic. At times, you will be driving through neighborhoods and towns. Please follow all speed limits and park only in areas that are both safe and legal. Most of all, enjoy your tour!

Modern highways make the trip across Occoquan Creek easier today than it was for the Federal army in June 1863. (dw)

Most of the stops along the tour routes have interpretation courtesy of Civil War Trails, a nonprofit educational organization dedicated to helping travelers connect with the sites and story of the Civil War.

"Maybe this *time* all this much to lose and all this much to gain: Pennsylvania, Maryland, the world, the golden dome of Washington itself to crown with desperate and unbelievable victory the desperate gamble, the cast made two years ago."

—*William Faulkner*

"The warrior-monument, crashed in fight,
Shall soar transfigured in loftier light,
A meaning ampler bear;
Soldier and priest with hymn and prayer
Have laid the stone, and every bone
Shall rest in honor there."

—*Herman Melville*

OVERLAY: The home of Lydia Leister on the Taneytown Road south of Gettysburg. General Meade used this house as his headquarters during most of the battle. (loc)

Prelude to the Campaign

May 1863. Union and Confederate forces caught their breath following their most recent clash at Chancellorsville. The battle was Gen. Robert E. Lee's finest hour during his first 11 months as commander of the Confederate Army of Northern Virginia. That sterling victory, however, came at an enormous cost. Confederate casualties from the battle totaled more than 13,000 men, including the famous, hard-fighting Thomas J. "Stonewall" Jackson. Losses for the Union Army of the Potomac were even higher at 17,000 men. Beyond the casualty list, army commander Maj. Gen. Joseph Hooker had performed far below expectations. With the first engagement of the spring campaign season over, and plenty of fair-weathered campaigning months ahead, high commands in both armies had to refocus on "what's next."

For Lee, that decision was already made: he wanted to go on the offensive and take the war northward out of Virginia. Despite his standing with Confederate President Jefferson Davis, Lee still had to successfully argue his position against a shifting Confederate strategy. After two trips to Richmond, Virginia, the capital of the Confederacy, and numerous conferences with Davis, Lee secured permission for a summer offensive into the Northern states. Lee argued against sending any of his men west to assist in the defense of Vicksburg. He argued that an offensive north near the Federal capital could possibly relieve Vicksburg by the Union pulling men north to deal with the invasion. Lt. Gen. John C. Pemberton would have to work with Gen. Joseph Johnston to deal with Generals Grant and Sherman.

During those meetings, Lee and Davis discussed the objectives for the proposed campaign. First, Lee was a general who constantly sought to maintain the strategic and tactical initiative. By maintaining the initiative he had earned at Chancellorsville, Lee forced his opponent to react to his movements.

One of the most beneficial objectives of Lee's summer

This tranquil modern image of Kelly's Ford belies the severe fight that occurred here in March 1863, as well as the numerous horsemen that splashed across the water during the battle of Brandy Station on June 9, 1863. (dw)

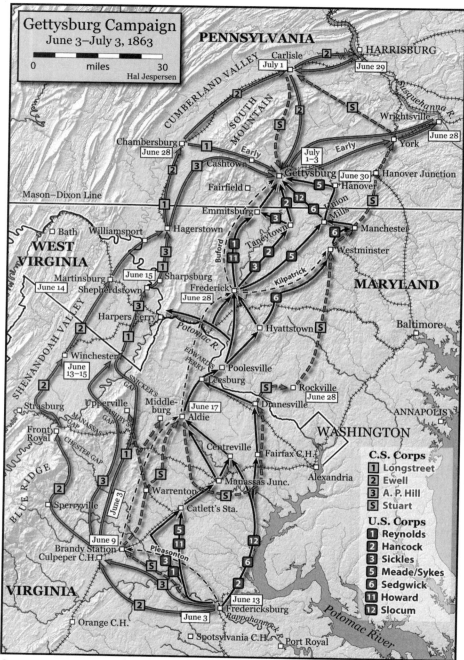

GETTYSBURG CAMPAIGN—The Gettysburg campaign kicked off on June 9 at the Battle of Brandy Station. Soon, Confederate infantry and cavalry began making their way north. Slow to react, the Federal Army of the Potomac began to move timidly north from Fredericksburg around June 13, unsure of the Confederate objective.

campaign would be to move the war out of Virginia. The general believed that his forward movement would lure the Army of the Potomac out of the state, following the Army of Northern Virginia. If this happened, the Commonwealth and its civilians would receive a respite from the hard hand of war. By 1863, Virginia had hosted several armies and had been the site for almost every major battle of the war in the east until that point. The landscape was not only altered by combat, but overburdened by trying to provide food, timber, water, and other natural resources to sustain the several maneuvering armies as well as its regular civilian population. With these forces removed from the state, the agricultural community would get an opportunity to plant and harvest their crops unmolested by military forces. Lee also would not need to rely on the Virginia countryside to feed his army during the invasion. He could provide food and fodder to his men and animals on the march and stock much-needed supplies for transport back to Virginia.

By June 1863, Gen. Robert E. Lee's ability as a military commander was already legendary. (loc)

Now was also the time to capitalize on the high morale of his army. This invasion, like the foray into Maryland nine months earlier, required a massive strain on the men in the ranks and the mechanisms that kept them moving forward. Only an army at its peak could handle such an arduous campaign. By the spring of 1863, the morale in the Army of Northern Virginia had never been higher. Their continual victories over the past year and their supreme faith in Lee enabled them to present an air of invincibility. Lee believed in this and so did his men in the ranks—and the planned invasion would capitalize on it.

Lt. Gen. Thomas J. "Stonewall" Jackson, wounded by his own men on May 2, 1863, died eight days later of complications from pneumonia. (loc)

Another objective for the invasion was to threaten major Northern metropolitan areas such as Washington, Baltimore, Harrisburg, or Philadelphia. Surely, the longer the Confederate army spent north of the famed Mason-Dixon Line, the more the Union's civilian populace would view the Lincoln administration's handling of the war in an even dimmer light. The capture or siege of a northern city, or a decisive victory over Hooker on northern ground, could encourage northern Peace Democrats to increase their efforts in Washington, gain even more political power, and apply pressure on the Lincoln administration to settle for peace with the Confederacy. Lee's time in the north could thus have serious political ramifications for Lincoln and the Republican Party, as well as the Union war effort on the whole.

All of Lee's immediate objectives and their possible degrees of success remained unseen until the campaign unfolded.

Maj. Gen. Joseph Hooker was the latest Union general defeated by Lee at the battle of Chancellorsville. His delayed response to Lee's movements brought much criticism to Washington. (loc)

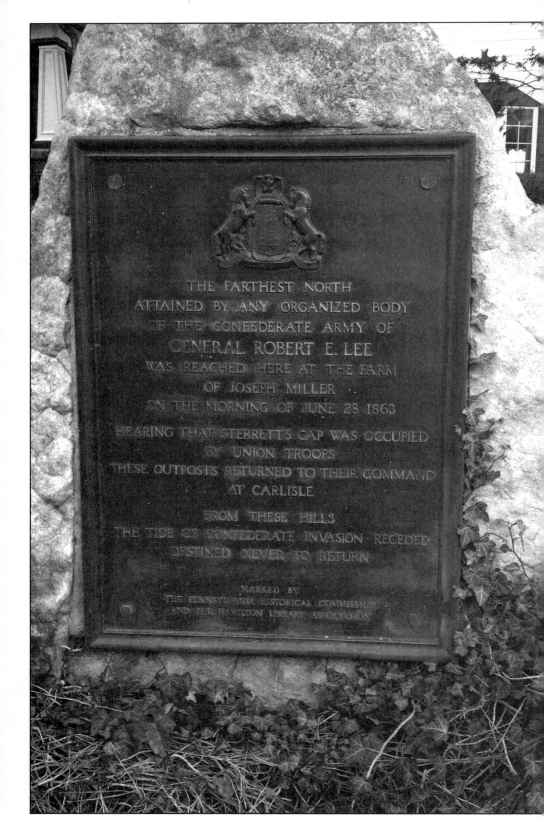

The Confederate Advance

CHAPTER ONE

This route will follow portions of the Army of Northern Virginia from Culpeper to Gettysburg. The marching routes of Hill's and Ewell's corps are highlighted. The entire route is approximately 167 miles.

The fight at Chancellorsville, May 1-6, 1863, took a terrible toll on the Army of Northern Virginia. Significant losses in men and officers had to be addressed. Lee wrote Maj. Gen. John B. Hood that the army would be "invincible if it could be properly organized and officered. There never were such men in an Army before. They will go anywhere and do anything if properly led. But there is the difficulty—proper commanders—where can they be obtained?"

Lee—who had contemplated for months various organizational challenges facing each branch of service—decided to divide the army into three corps with three divisions each, instead of the previous structure of two very large corps. Lt. Gen. James Longstreet retained command of the First Corps, while both Richard S. Ewell and Ambrose P. Hill were promoted to lieutenant generalships: Ewell to command Jackson's old corps, and Hill to command the newly-created Third Corps. Hill's Corps was composed of one division from each of the original two corps, plus, a newly created division. The artillery and cavalry branches received similar reorganization.

The two new commanders led many to wonder

This monument, in Carlisle Springs, Pennsylvania, marks the northernmost point the Confederates reached during the Gettysburg Campaign. (cm)

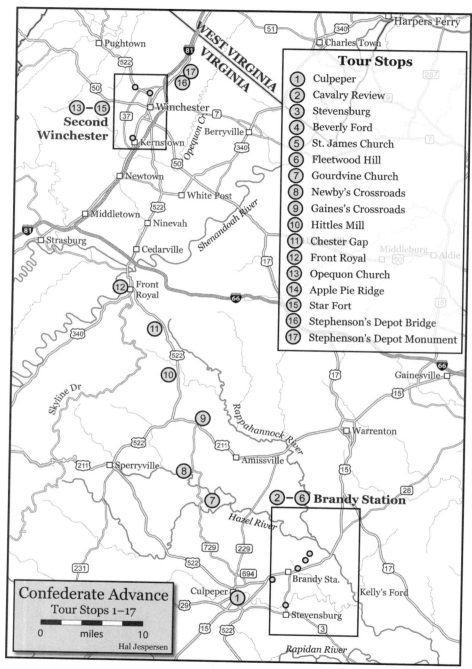

Tour Stops

1. Culpeper
2. Cavalry Review
3. Stevensburg
4. Beverly Ford
5. St. James Church
6. Fleetwood Hill
7. Gourdvine Church
8. Newby's Crossroads
9. Gaines's Crossroads
10. Hittles Mill
11. Chester Gap
12. Front Royal
13. Opequon Church
14. Apple Pie Ridge
15. Star Fort
16. Stephenson's Depot Bridge
17. Stephenson's Depot Monument

Confederate Advance
Tour Stops 1–17

0   miles   10

Hal Jespersen

CONFEDERATE ADVANCE—The driving route will follow the action around Brandy Station on June 9 and primarily follow the route of Lt. Gen. Richard Ewell's Corps northward to Winchester.

LEFT: Maj. Gen. John Bell Hood, more than any other officer, had molded the Texas Brigade into the hard-hitting unit it had become known as by the time of the Gettysburg campaign. Now, Hood commanded a division in General Longstreet's First Corps. (loc)

RIGHT: Commander of the Army of Northern Virginia's First Corps, Lt. Gen. James Longstreet became Lee's most trusted subordinate. (loc)

about their ability to handle a corps on campaign and in the field. Previously, the army's field leadership had always been in the hands of Longstreet and Jackson, two corps commanders who had already proven themselves. Ewell had not commanded troops in the field since his wounding at Second Manassas in August 1862. Hill, meanwhile, had performed well during the war, although he and Jackson had had differences that affected Hill's reputation in the army.

Increasing the overall size of the army was also a concern. Would Lee have enough wagons to secure food and forage while living off the land or to transport sick and wounded? How was the health of his service animals—could they make the journey northward? Lee worked methodically through each concern, and for better or for worse, this was the army that Lee ordered forward on June 3 1863, to start the Gettysburg campaign.

The Confederate Advance tour begins in Culpeper, Virginia, at the Culpeper Museum. The museum is located in the circa.1904 train station (the current train station, meanwhile, is on the location of the war-time station). The museum interprets the history of Culpeper and contains significant information on the Civil War history of the area. In June 1863, Culpeper was vital to Lee as a jumping-off point for his movement north. The town was strategically located along the Orange and Alexandria Railroad and near mountain gaps that led toward the Shenandoah Valley. The museum is located at 113 South Commerce Street, Culpeper, Virginia 22701.

GPS: N 38°.4723012 W 77°.9936231

LEFT: Commander of the Army of Northern Virginia's Second Corps—and the replacement for the fallen Jackson— Lt. Gen. Richard S. Ewell led the advance into Maryland and Pennsylvania. (loc)

RIGHT: Lt. Gen. A.P. Hill commanded the Army of Northern Virginia's newly created Third Corps. (loc)

STOP 1: CULPEPER MUSEUM / TRAIN STATION

The Gettysburg campaign began on Wednesday, June 3, when Lee ordered the divisions of Maj. Gens. Lafayette McLaws and John B. Hood towards Culpeper Court House. "I commenced to draw the army from the vicinity of Fredericksburg on Wednesday morning," Lee wrote to President Davis days later, describing the opening scene.

For the early stages of the campaign, Lee planned to leave Gen. Hill's Third Corps in Fredericksburg to monitor Federal activity across the Rappahannock River and hold the attention of Hooker. Meanwhile, the two corps under Longstreet and Ewell would push westward beyond the Federal right flank and towards the Shenandoah. Lee wanted to use the Valley and the Blue Ridge Mountains to screen his movements from the prying eyes of Union intelligence. It would also allow him to act on his stated objective of clearing the

A sketch by renowned Civil War artist Alfred Waud, "Shelling the rebel rifle pits on the Rappahannock--previous to the third crossing of Sedgwicks corps June 5th." (loc)

Valley of the Federal forces that had been operating in the area since the winter of 1862-1863. The first stop along this route was a general concentration of the Confederate marching column at Culpeper Court House. The Confederate cavalry was already concentrated in the area near Brandy Station, watching the Rappahannock River fords and waiting on Lee's planned movement.

The following day, June 4, Maj. Gen. Robert Rodes's division of the Second Corps was on the move, while the last two divisions of the corps, Maj. Gens. Jubal Early and Edward Johnson, broke camp on Friday, June 5. With large portions of the Confederate army in motion and a line that stretched from Culpeper Court House to Fredericksburg, it was a dangerous time for Lee and the Confederate army if Hooker caught wind of Lee's movements.

Known as "Uncle John" by his men, Maj. Gen. John Sedgwick commanded the VI Corps in the Army of the Potomac during the Gettysburg campaign. His men were tasked with crossing the Rappahannock River to gain further intelligence on Confederate movements in the early days of June 1863. (loc)

With numerous signs that Confederates had abandoned large stretches of their earthworks—including clouds of dust from marching columns and decreased numbers on the front lines—Hooker ordered Union Maj. Gen. John Sedgwick to make a reconnaissance-in-force across the Rappahannock River. Lee, in his letter to President Davis on June 7, recorded the action: "After driving back our sharpshooters, under a furious cannonade from their batteries, by a force of skirmishers, they crossed a small body of troops, and occupied the back of the river." The probe across the river stopped the Confederate marching column in its tracks as "I [Lee] thought it prudent to . . . halt his march [Ewell] until I could see what the next day would develop." However, the Federal army stirred little, and Confederate columns resumed their march.

A wartime image of Culpeper Court House, Virginia. Culpeper suffered constantly throughout the war from marching and encamping armies. (loc)

By June 7, General Ewell's three divisions reached Culpeper Court House. General Rodes reached the Court House proper, while divisions under generals Johnson and Early were within three miles—a close supporting distance. More Confederate units were on the march on June 8, and

Famed and feared Confederate cavalryman Maj. Gen. James Ewell Brown "Jeb" Stuart played a controversial role in the Gettysburg campaign that is still debated today. (loc)

by day's close, five Confederate divisions were within the vicinity with more on the way.

Return to Main Street and take a right (north). Main Street will become Brandy Road. Travel for 4.3 miles and you will see a Virginia State Police office on the left. Turn in and pull into the first parking lot on the left. It is in this vicinity near the railroad that Maj. Gen. J. E. B. Stuart hosted his grand reviews. The fields behind the police station (where modern day Route 29 runs) are where the reviews took place. At the time of the war, this farm was owned by notable Unionist John Minor Botts, whose home still stands on Auburn Road (private property). This stop does not have an interpretive marker.

GPS: N 38 °.49242 W 77 °.925789

STOP 2: CAVALRY REVIEW SITE

On June 8, 1863, Maj. Gen. J. E. B. Stuart hosted a grand review. It was the third such event in as many weeks. Noted Confederate attendees included Lee, Longstreet, and Ewell. Former cavalryman Gen. Hood also received an invitation to attend and to bring "any of his friends." Hood complied and brought not only his staff but the other 8,000 "friends" from his division. The general was heard to quip to Brig. Gen. W. H. Fitzhugh Lee, the officer who had extended the invitation, "You invited me and my people and you see I've brought them."

One participant recalled of the third review, "It was a splendid military parade . . . with men and horses groomed their best, and the command arrayed with military precision, with colors flying, bugles sounding, and with regimental and brigade officers in proper positions." Another eyewitness to the day, Capt. William W. Blackford,

recalled Stuart's command on June 8 as being "at its zenith of power." However, the following day, June 9, severely tested that notion.

Turn left out of the state police entrance

Site of the second and third reviews of Stuart's cavalrymen. Today, the Virginia State Police office and Rt. 29 sit in the middle of the fields where the Confederate cavalry formed. (dw)

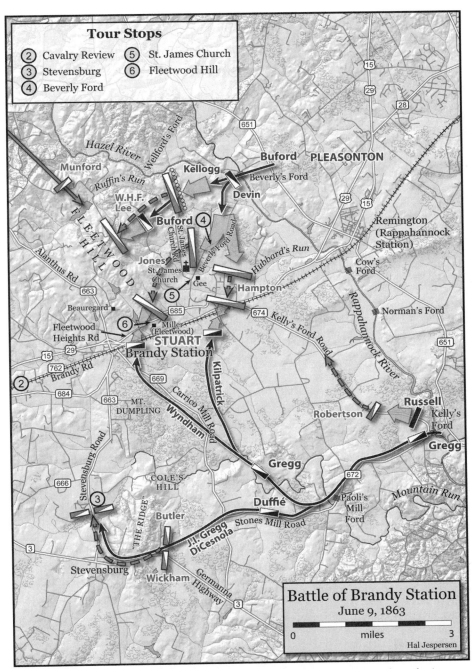

Tour Stops

② Cavalry Review   ⑤ St. James Church
③ Stevensburg   ⑥ Fleetwood Hill
④ Beverly Ford

Battle of Brandy Station
June 9, 1863

0   miles   3

Hal Jespersen

BATTLE OF BRANDY STATION—In early June, Maj. Gen. Joe Hooker ordered Federal cavalry to cross the Rappahannock near Brandy Station and move against the Confederate cavalry reported to be near Culpeper Courthouse. Their mission: to discover Confederate intentions and destroy the legendary Southern cavalry.

road onto Brandy Road. Travel for 1.9 miles into Brandy Station and make a right onto Route 669 (Carrico Mills Road). Then make your immediate right onto Route 663 (Stevensburg Road). Remain on Stevensburg Road for 3.4 miles and make a left into Lenn Park. There are several interpretive displays here discussing the Civil War actions in the area and a monument to William Farley, who was killed in this area during the battle. Wartime Stevensburg is approximately one mile further along Stevensburg Road.

GPS: N 38 °.455477 W 77 °.900634

STOP 3: BATTLE OF BRANDY STATION: STEVENSBURG

Hooker received reports that a large Confederate force was massing in Culpeper on his western (right) flank. Hooker interpreted this presence as a possible raid on his supply lines and directed Army of the Potomac cavalry commander Maj. Gen. Alfred Pleasonton to attack the Confederate cavalry in Culpeper in order to disperse and destroy it.

The plan called for a two-pronged attack launched early on June 9. Brigadier General John Buford would lead his division across the Rappahannock River at Beverly's Ford, while the cavalry division under Brig. Gen. David Gregg would cross at Kelly's Ford. Each was to approach Culpeper from a different direction, enveloping the Confederate cavalry. Unknown to Pleasonton, the Confederate cavalry was not in Culpeper but much closer to the Rappahannock River—at Brandy Station—and the force was also much larger than originally expected.

Gregg was supposed to cross at Kelly's Ford in coordination with Buford's advance. However,

LEFT: **By the time of the Gettysburg campaign, Maj. Gen. Alfred Pleasonton was a newly minted major general in charge of the Cavalry Corps of the Army of the Potomac. His inflated reports during the battle of Chancellorsville helped him achieve this promotion from Gen. Hooker, Army of the Potomac's commanding general.** (loc)

RIGHT: **Brig. Gen. John Buford took command of a new division following the promotion of Gen. Pleasonton. Buford led attacks at Brandy Station and Upperville during the Gettysburg campaign, and later opened the battle at Gettysburg on July 1, 1863.** (loc)

LEFT: Frenchmen and Crimean War veteran Col. Alfred Duffié resigned his military post in France in 1859 and moved to the United States. The experienced officer joined the Union war effort in 1861. Because of his poor performance during the battle of Brandy Station, he was demoted from division command and placed back in command of his previous regiment, the 1st Rhode Island Cavalry. (loc)

Gregg's cavalry crossed Kelly's Ford two hours late because one of his divisions, that of Col. Alfred N. Duffié, got lost. When the lost Federal troopers finally arrived, the two units crossed the river and pushed on towards Stevensburg without any opposition. Just before arriving there, Gregg and the majority of his division left the road and changed direction towards Brandy Station—all according to the battle plan for the day, albeit late.

RIGHT: Brig. Gen. David McMurtrie Gregg was not new to division command when the Federal cavalry were reorganized following Pleasonton's promotion. Officially in the role as a division commander since February 1863, Gregg's troopers fought at Brandy Station, Aldie, Middleburg, Upperville, and Gettysburg during the campaign. (loc)

The remainder of Gregg's wing proceeded towards Stevensburg, commanded by Duffié. The colonel's orders were to protect the Federal cavalry's flank while, at the same time, support the advance on Culpeper, the ultimate Federal goal. Duffié encountered resistance from the 2nd South Carolina and the 4th Virginia Cavalry where the Old Carolina Road crossed Mountain Run. Eventually, Federal forces pushed the Carolinians and Virginians aside, but not soon enough to reach Brandy Station or Fleetwood Hill to be of any material assistance during the much larger battle that erupted there. Duffié's delays earlier that morning and here at Mountain Run had a substantial impact on the outcome at Brandy Station.

Just east of here you can see Hansborough Ridge, which played a major role in the June 9th action. It was also the location of the Union II Corps's winter encampment during the winter of 1863-1864.

Turn right out of the park entrance and retrace your route to Brandy Station. Once back on Brandy Road, take a right onto Route 663 (Alanthus Road). Then make your immediate right onto Route

Heros von Borcke, a Prussian cavalry officer, arrived in Charleston, South Carolina, via a blockade runner in the spring of 1862. By May of that year, he was assigned to Gen. Stuart by order of the Confederate secretary of war. Von Borcke became a close aide and confidant of Stuart. He was severely wounded in the neck during the battle of Middleburg. (f3)

685 (Fleetwood Heights Road). In 1.7 miles, make a left onto Cobbs Legion Road, then your immediate left onto Route 676 (Beverly Ford Road). After 1.2 miles, turn left into the parking area (you will see several interpretive signs). At this stop, there is an interpretive trail established by the Civil War Trust covering the action at Beverly's Ford and Buford's Knoll. Route 676 follows the original wartime road to Beverly's Ford. During your drive to this stop, you will pass by many Civil War Trails stops; we will return to all of these later. The tour is designed to cover the battle of Brandy Station in chronological order.

GPS: N 38 °.531475 W 77 °.858334

STOP 4: BATTLE OF BRANDY STATION: BEVERLY FORD

As morning fog and dew blanketed Stuart's command, the sound of a Sharps carbine broke the morning stillness. Within moments, Buford's cavalry splashed across Beverly Ford, initiating the first moments of what became the largest cavalry battle during the American Civil War. Slowing them down, a thin line of pickets from the 6th Virginia Cavalry held fast, but the overwhelming numbers of Federals pushed the Virginians away from the riverbank. Buford's troopers then moved beyond the picket line and the ford crossing before surprising another element of the 6th Virginia.

Major Johann August Heinrich Heros von Borcke, riding with General Stuart and acting as a staff officer, recalled those early morning moments: "Stuart was immediately awakened, the alarm sounded throughout the entire headquarters; negro servants saddled the horses, and everything was made ready for the imminent fight. A few minutes later Stuart's couriers raced off to wake

A *Harpers Weekly* woodcut titled "Buford's Charge at Brandy Station" dramatically illustrates troopers under Buford's command during their fight against Stuart's vaunted cavaliers on June 9, 1863. (loc)

A modern day view towards Beverly Ford, where Buford's command crossed the river and attacked the Confederate position on the opposite bank. (dw)

the troops. . . ." Another German officer serving on Stuart's staff, Captain Justus Scheibert also recalled the early start to the fight. "On June 9, around 3:30 in the morning, we were suddenly roused from our slumber by couriers racing up excitedly. We had been sleeping in our tent, partially dressed as usual. They reported that our pickets on the Rappahannock had been surprised by the enemy."

Turn right out of the parking lot onto Route 676 (Beverly's Ford Road). In 0.8 miles, turn right onto Route 676 (St. James Church Road) and the parking area is immediately to your left. The Civil War Trust owns and protects a large portion of the battlefield in this area. The site of St. James Church is preserved by the Brandy Station Foundation and is located another 0.25 miles down Route 676. The walking trail for this portion of the battlefield is across the road from the parking area.

GPS: N 38 °.521686 W 77 °.865943

STOP 5: BATTLE OF BRANDY STATION: ST. JAMES CHURCH

Nearly to St. James Church, Federal troopers from New York and Illinois almost captured the bulk of the Confederate horse artillery parked nearby. If it wasn't for the able work of Capt. J. F. Hart, who managed to wheel two of his guns into position and open fire on the advancing horsemen while the rest of the battalion was pulled to the rear, a damaging blow to Confederate material and morale could have occurred.

The size of the fight grew as more Confederate troopers, mostly undressed and riding without proper saddles and equipment, arrived on scene. The 7th Virginia Cavalry commanded by Lt. Col. Thomas Marshall, was the first to assist its sister regiment and Hart's two guns, materially slowing Buford's thrust. The work of the 7th provided enough time for the rest of the brigade, commanded by Brig. Gen. William "Grumble" Jones, to arrive, as well as reinforcements from Brig. Gens. Wade Hampton and W. H. Fitzhugh Lee.

The Confederate reaction to Buford's morning assault was quick and confident. By 10:00 a.m., the weight of Confederate reinforcements brought Buford's assault to a halt. Soon, the majority of the

Brig. Gen. William "Grumble" Jones's brigade of Confederate troopers rejoined Stuart's command in time for the fierce fight at Brandy Station. Throughout June 1863, his men protected the rear of the Army of Northern Virginia during its advance northward. (phocw)

Better known as "Rooney" by friends and family, Brig. Gen. W.H.F. Lee, the second son of Gen. Lee, rose through the ranks of the Confederate cavalry after being placed under Stuart's command in 1862. "Rooney" was wounded during the fight at Brandy Station, later captured during his recuperation by Union soldiers, and not exchanged until February 1864. (loc)

Brig. Gen. Wade Hampton had raised and financed a unit known as "Hampton's Legion" at the outset of war. By June 1863, Hampton had participated in many of the theater's fiercest battles. He received a slight wound during the battle of Brandy Station, but his brother was mortally wounded there. (loc)

Grandson of Supreme Court Justice John Marshall, Lt. Col. Thomas Marshall of the 7th Virginia Cavalry had served as an aide to "Stonewall Jackson" during the battle of First Manassas in July 1861. (loc)

Confederates left the St. James Church area; a new threat was now facing Stuart back at Fleetwood Hill.

Turn right out of the parking area and right onto Route 676. In 0.4 miles, take a right onto Cobbs Legion Road, then a right onto Route 685 (Fleetwood Heights Road). In 0.8 miles, turn left into the parking area for Fleetwood Hill. This area was preserved and the landscape restored in 2015 by the Civil War Trust. A walking trail located here interprets the action on June 9, 1863, in more detail.

GPS: N 38 °.509609 W 77 °.879459

Stop 6: Battle of Brandy Station: Fleetwood Hill

Stuart recalled Hampton's and Jones's commands and directed them towards Fleetwood Hill to face the threat of Gregg's wing coming up from Kelly's Ford. The first Federals to attack Fleetwood from the south were under Col. Percy Wyndham, striking the lightly defended Fleetwood about 11:00 a.m. Confederates from the St. James Church front arrived just in time to blunt Wyndham's attack, but the threat was not over. Col. Judson Kilpatrick's brigade arrived from the southeast and temporarily took the heights. Several spirited charges by both sides eventually led to the Federals calling off further attacks. Around 3:00 p.m., along the northern portions of Fleetwood Hill near Yew Ridge, Confederate cavalry under Brig. Gen. "Rooney" Lee and Col. Tom Munford held off a spirited attack by Buford.

After 14 hours of fighting, the Federals—with no more forces to commit—pulled back and re-crossed the Rappahannock. They also received reports that there might be Confederate infantry in the area. "Thus ended one of the greatest cavalry battles of modern times," said Maj. Heros von Borcke. The cost to Union and Confederate forces at Brandy Station was high. The casualties of both sides demonstrated the ferocity of the fight. Confederate losses amounted to 51 killed, 250 wounded, and 132 missing. Union losses numbered 484 killed and wounded combined and 372 listed as prisoners of war.

Having served in both French and English military units, Col. Percy Wyndham arrived in the United States in late 1861 and immediately joined the Union war effort. Captured in June 1862 and soon released, Wyndham fought and was wounded during the fight at Brandy Station. (loc)

The battle at Brandy Station had far-reaching implications. Speaking of the fight years after the war, Stuart's staff officer, Maj. H. B. McClellan wrote, "one result of incalculable importance did follow this battle,—it made the Federal cavalry." Despite Stuart's congratulatory order to his men in which he claimed the battle a victory, it was anything but the kind of victory that the Southern cavaliers were used to, and several officers in the Army of Northern Virginia questioned the claim. Most notable was General McLaws. Writing his wife Emily on June 10, 1863, McLaws noted that "our cavalry were surprised yesterday by the enemy and had to do some desperate fighting to retrieve the day." Of the notion that Stuart's men pushed the Federal cavalry back across the Rappahannock, McLaws wrote, "The enemy were not however driven back but retired at their leisure, having accomplished I suppose what they intended."

A modern view looking towards Fleetwood Hill, which dominates the terrain around the Brandy Station battlefield. (dw)

But *did* the Federal cavalry achieve their objective as laid out by Hooker: the destruction and dispersion of the Confederate cavalry under Stuart? When Stuart and the Confederate cavalry crossed the

Rappahannock just days after the fight and began to screen the movements of the Confederate infantry as they approached the Shenandoah Valley, clearly Pleasonton and the Federal cavalry had in fact not accomplished their main objective.

Turn left out of the parking area. Notice, across the road, the brick house on the hill in the distance. This is Beauregard, where Lee watched a portion of the battle of Brandy Station. Drive 1 mile, make a left onto Route 663 (Alanthus Road), then your immediate right onto Route 29/15. In 2.5 miles, take the exit for Route 15 Business. Travel 2.5 miles and take a right onto Route 694 (Ira Hoffman Lane). Continue on Ira Hoffman Lane for 1.6 miles and cross Route 229, continuing on Route 729 (Eggbornsville Road). Travel for 9.8 miles and the Gourdvine Baptist Church will be on your right. This road is the wartime "Richmond Road," used by the majority of the Army of Northern Virginia, which ran from Culpeper to Front Royal. Little has changed in this rural landscape.

GPS: N 38 °.606469 W 78 °.056604

STOP 7: GOURDVINE BAPTIST CHURCH

The Gourdvine Baptist Church was established in 1791; the current building was built in 1838. After the battle of Brandy Station, Lee evaluated the situation and concluded that the action at Brandy Station had no impact on his plans to move the army north. Stuart remained at Brandy Station for a time while recuperating and reorganizing the cavalry. Lee directed Ewell's Corps to lead the advance. Ewell moved north from Culpeper through Rappahannock County and through Chester Gap into the Shenandoah Valley. The Richmond Road was used by Rodes's division as Early's and Johnson's divisions used the Sperryville Turnpike (modern day Route 522) to Sperryville. Hill's Corps followed Longstreet's Corps. They used many of these same roads.

Here at Gourdvine, Rodes camped on June 10 before moving northward toward Chester Gap. "Lee and his army passed right by our gate on his way to and from Pennsylvania," John Moffett wrote after the war. "I remember how anxious the families were that I should see him (Lee)." Living

Gourdvine Baptist Church. Founded in the 1790s, the current building was built in the 1830s with 20th century additions. (ro)

near Gourdvine, Moffett and other members of the church saw many Confederates that summer and then later in July on their return from Gettysburg.

Turn right out of the parking lot and continue north on Route 729 (Richmond Road). This road was used by Confederates on their way to and from Gettysburg. The modern road runs a little east of the historic road once you pass the Thornton River. Take the Richmond Road for 4.1 miles to Newby's Crossroads. There will be a small pull-off on the right with three Civil War Trails signs.

GPS: N 38 °.649297 W 78 °.074776

STOP 8: NEWBY'S CROSSROADS

Newby's Crossroads was an important local crossroads named after the Newby family (their home still stands across the road and is private property). Gen. Rodes's division continued its march through here on June 11, and a week later Longstreet's Corps with Gen. Lee marched through this area. After Gettysburg, much of the Confederate army also marched through here heading south.

The markers here tell the story of the Gettysburg campaign and the sad story of Dangerfield Newby (whose family lived nearby), a freed slave who was the first raider

At Newby's Crossroads, the Richmond Road passed by the Newby farm. The modern-day driveway to the Newby House is the original road bed of the Richmond Road. (ro)

killed during John Brown's Raid at Harpers Ferry.

The house on the hill to your right was the home of the Newby family. The driveway is the war-time path of the Richmond Road to Gourdvine Church. Turn around and take Route 729 (Richmond Road) north (a left turn). In about 2.5 miles, you will go up a steep hill. Many Confederates noted this hill during their march, and many men fell out in this area due to the steep grade and hot conditions. Continue north another 2.5 miles and turn left into the parking area in front of a landscape business. There are two Civil War Trails markers facing the highway.

GPS: N 38 °.718723 W 78 °.067161

STOP 9: GAINES'S CROSSROADS

Gaines's Crossroads was a busy place in June 1863. Over the next several weeks, the majority of the infantry of the Army of Northern Virginia passed through this crossroads. Rodes marched through here on June 11 headed northward towards Flint Hill. Early's and Johnson's divisions used the Sperryville Turnpike from Culpeper to Sperryville and then marched east from Sperryville to Gaines's Crossroads to continue their march northward behind Rodes. Early attempted a shortcut from Little Washington to Flint Hill along the Fodderstack Road, but his artillery and wagon train could not overcome the steep inclines and narrow road. He was forced to go back to Little Washington and then march to Gaines's Crossroads.

A week later, Hill's and Longstreet's corps marched north through here. Just north of the crossroads is Grimsley Road, where Longstreet and Lee split off from Richmond Road and marched to Markham. Hill followed Ewell's route to Chester Gap. Across the highway is Ben Venue and its rare street of original, brick slave quarters. Ewell used the main house as his headquarters.

Dangerfield Newby, a freed slave killed during John Brown's raid at Harpers Ferry, had joined Brown in an effort to free his wife enslaved in Prince William County. (loc)

Retrace your route to where you entered the parking lot. Take a left onto Route 729 (Richmond Road) and go straight across

Route 211. You are still on the Richmond Road, but today it's called Ben Venue Road. After 1.2 miles you will see Grimsley Road on your right. Longstreet's Corps took this road to Markham and Manassas Gap. Continue straight on Ben Venue Road for 2.3 miles into Flint Hill. Take a right on Route 522 (Zachary Taylor Highway) and drive 2.3 miles, make a left into the parking area and look for the Civil War Trails sign.

GPS: N 38 °.791822 W 78 °.104582

The Ben Venue Slave cabins are a rare example of enslaved community architecture. Nearby stands the main house of Ben Venue that Lt. Gen. Ewell used as his headquarters. (ro)

SIDE TRIP: EARLY'S SHORTCUT TO FLINT HILL

If you are interested in taking Fodderstack Road, where Early attempted a shortcut to Flint Hill, turn west on Route 211. Drive 5 miles, then take a right onto Route Business 211 (Warren Avenue). This will take you into Little Washington. At 0.4 miles, take a right onto Main Street; this will become Fodderstack Road. This road follows the same path that Early's division tried to take to get from Little Washington to Flint Hill. Early believed it was a shortcut and could possibly avoid a logjam at Gaines's Crossroads. Early was not able to traverse the entire road and had to double back to Little Washington. Today you can take the road all the way to Flint Hill (5.5 miles) and turn left onto Route 522 (Zachary Taylor Highway). In 2.1 miles, turn left into the parking area and look for the Civil War Trails sign.

GPS: N 38 °.791822 W 78 °.104582

STOP 10: HITTLES MILL

As Rodes's division cleared the village of Flint Hill, he ordered his men into camp on the evening of June 11. Rodes believed that Early's division was now in front of him, so he decided to camp just north of Flint Hill. Soon Rodes discovered that Early's attempt at a shortcut from Little Washington had not been successful and that Early was still behind him. To allow room for the Confederate column to pass, Rodes ordered his men to break camp and move north, where they camped at Hittles Mill.

On the morning of June 12, Ewell arrived from

Gaines's Crossroads to meet with Rodes to discuss strategy. The previous day, Ewell had met with Generals Early and Johnson to explain Lee's overall strategy for the upcoming campaign. This meeting took place near the area known as Sandy Hook. Ewell rode to the meeting in a buggy, and he requested that Rodes join him. (Ewell had lost his leg a year earlier at Second Manassas and still faced complications with riding on horseback). Following the meeting, the two men rode to Front Royal together in Ewell's carriage and continued to discuss the numerous objectives that Lee had for the campaign.

Turn left out of the parking lot and continue north on Route 522 for 5.1 miles and take a left onto Chester Gap Road. After 0.1 miles, you will see two Civil War Trails markers on the right. You are now in Chester Gap.

GPS: N 38 °.861968 W 78 °.131772

STOP 11: CHESTER GAP

Chester Gap was used throughout the war by both sides as a way to access the Shenandoah Valley. On June 12, the lead elements of the Army of Northern Virginia under Rodes crossed the gap, and Ewell's entire corps moved through the gap on the way to Front Royal. Many veterans of Stonewall Jackson's 1862 Shenandoah Valley campaign were excited to be returning to the Valley. Sgt. Daniel Sheetz of the 2nd Virginia Infantry wrote his fiancé Lydia Philips, "I must tell you we were glad to get back to the Valley again."

Several days later, Hill's Corps marched through here, as well. North Carolina troops under Hill camping in the gap encountered a den of rattlesnakes, which many considered to be a bad omen.

Continue north on Chester Gap Road, then make a left onto Route 522 (Remount Road). Route 522 will take you into Front Royal and become Commerce Street. After 5 miles, take a left onto Main St. The Front Royal-Warren County Visitor Center will be on the right (414 East Main Street, Front Royal, Virginia 22630). There are two Civil War Trails signs in front of the visitor center.

There are several historic sites and museums in Front Royal that relate to the Civil War, as well as several Civil War Trails signs

An 1862 Edwin Forbes sketch of Chester Gap, which served as a main thoroughfare into the Shenandoah Valley throughout the war. (loc)

that explain events related to the 1862 battle of Front Royal and Col. John S. Mosby's actions in the area. The visitor center has information on all of these sites.

GPS: N 38 °.917732 W 78 °.189292

STOP 12: FRONT ROYAL

Because the battle of Brandy Station delayed Stuart's departure from Culpeper, Lee ordered the 1,600 strong cavalry brigade (officially labeled "mounted infantry") under Brig. Gen. Albert G. Jenkins to rendezvous with Rodes in Front Royal. Jenkins served as cavalry support for Ewell's Corps as it dealt with the Federal forces in Winchester and Berryville. Jenkins's cavalry were from western Virginia and were not as disciplined or well-trained as Stuart's cavalrymen, nor were they armed with conventional cavalry weapons.

Though the Confederate advance was secret, local citizens realized something was afoot when pontoon boats arrived on June 11, a few days before the arrival of Ewell's Corps. As the Confederates entered south of town, they continued northward and crossed the Shenandoah River—which was low, so the early pontoon bridges were not needed—and camped just north of Front Royal at Cedarville. Local citizens lined the streets to welcome the Confederate army back to the Shenandoah Valley.

At Cedarville, Ewell met with his division commanders and laid out the plans to deal with the Federal garrisons at Winchester and Berryville. The corps commander stressed the importance of swift action, to rid the Valley of the Federals quickly and to keep the Army of the Potomac (which was still near Fredericksburg) from catching up and blocking

Brig. Gen. Albert Jenkins's Civil War career moved between the political and military realms. During the Gettysburg campaign, his command served as a cavalry screen for the Confederate Second Corps. (loc)

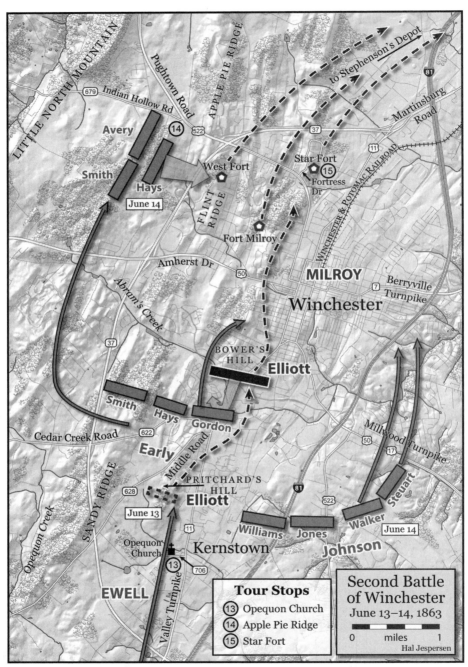

SECOND BATTLE OF WINCHESTER—As the Confederate infantry under Lt. Gen. Richard Ewell approached Winchester, the indecisive Federal commander, Maj. Gen. Robert Milroy, left his outnumbered forces in Winchester. Relying on their strong fortifications, the Federals soon faced nearly three times their number of Confederates.

Lee's invasion. Ewell ordered Johnson's and Early's divisions to take on Maj. Gen. Robert Milroy in Winchester. Meanwhile Rodes and Jenkins's cavalry would head east to Berryville to deal with the small Federal force there, then head to Martinsburg to cut off Milroy's retreat from Winchester.

Continue on Main Street and make a right on Route 340 (North Royal Street). In 1.4 miles, stay right onto Route 340/522 (North Shenandoah Avenue). In 3.1 miles, you will drive through the no-longer existent Cedarville. Here, Ewell's Corps encamped on June 12, and then launched its attack on Milroy at Winchester. Continue another 6.3 miles and take a left onto Route 277 (Fairfax Pike). Near here, Early split off and marched west to reach the Valley Turnpike while Johnson continued northward toward Winchester. We will be following Early's general route. Follow Route 277 for 4.7 miles into Stephen's City (wartime name of Newtown). Turn right onto Route 11 (Main Street); you are now on the Valley Turnpike. Stay on Route 11 for 4.3 miles to Kernstown. Turn left onto Route 706 (Opequon Church Lane). At the end of the street is a cul de sac in front of Opequon Presbyterian Church. The interpretive markers here talk about the action in 1862, but this area provides a good vantage point to start the Second Battle of Winchester.

GPS: N 39°.140015 W 78°.194670

STOP 13: SECOND BATTLE OF WINCHESTER: OPEQUON PRESBYTERIAN CHURCH

Rodes's division accompanied the rest of the corps as it moved toward Berryville and Martinsburg, then peeled away as ordered by Ewell. The other two divisions, Early's and Johnson's, arrived at Kernstown from the south and deployed in the area of Pritchard's Hill just to the north. Ewell's plan to attack Winchester, which was defended by 8,000 Federal soldiers under Maj. Gen. Robert H. Milroy's command, was to send Johnson's division eastward along the Front Royal Road toward the town. Meanwhile, Early and his division would head west before turning north and eventually attack Milroy's position from the west. General Milroy's plan for defending against the Confederate assault was the faith that he had in his defensive positions: a series of forts and heights along

This view from Apple Pie Ridge of West Fort (in the distant tree line) represents the direction that Confederate forces under Brig. Gen. Harry Hay's Louisianans attacked on June 14th.. (dw)

the southern, western, and northwestern approaches to the town.

As Ewell looked further into the situation in and around Winchester, the first shots for the contested town were fired. Federal soldiers from the 87th Pennsylvania, 13th Pennsylvania Cavalry, and Battery L, 5th United States Artillery ambushed the 1st Maryland and 14th Virginia Cavalry near Kernstown. The Union contingent—more than 600 officers and men under the command of Col. Edwin Schall—was led well that day but roughly handled by the Rebel infantry. The opening shots of the battle had taken place south of Winchester.

The battle continued the following day, June 13. A brigade of Federal soldiers and artillery under the command of Brig. Gen. Washington Elliott deployed on and to the west and east of Pritchard's Hill directly in front of you. Brigadier General Harry Hays's Louisiana Tigers advanced first over the hill itself. Near 4:00 p.m., Brig. Gen. John Gordon's Georgians advanced on the Tigers's left. Although the attack made progress and pushed Elliott's command begrudgingly rearward, the Confederates fell into chaos and confusion. The two Confederate brigades bivouacked on the field that evening while rain soaked the area. That night, Elliott received orders from Milroy to fall back to the forts ringing Winchester. The fight for Winchester in this area was over.

A period sketch, "View of Winchester, Va., from fort on the hill N.E. of the town." The town of Winchester saw three battles in its environs and changed hands dozens of times during the war. (loc)

If you are interested in visiting Pritchard's Hill, return to Route 11 and take a left. Drive 0.3 miles and make a left onto Battle Park Drive. At the end of the street is the entrance to Pritchard's Hill Battlefield. This land is preserved and managed by the Kernstown Battlefield Association and is open seasonally. Please do not trespass if the gates are closed.

GPS: N 39 °.143955 W 78 °.192356—Pritchard's Hill Battlefield

Return to Route 11 (Valley Pike) and turn right, then take the right exit onto Route 37 north/west. Travel 6.4 miles and take the exit for Route 522 (North Frederick Pike). Take a left at the bottom of the exit ramp onto Route 522 West. In 0.7 miles, take a left onto Route 679 (Indian Hollow Road). The Civil War Trails marker is on the right in the parking lot for the produce stand.

Brig. Gen. Harry T. Hays, a brigade commander in the Second Corps, led the famed hard-hitting Louisiana Tigers into battle at Second Winchester, and again at Gettysburg on July 1 and 2. (loc)

GPS: N 39 °.214956 W 78 °.191603—Apple Pie Ridge

STOP 14: SECOND BATTLE OF WINCHESTER: APPLE PIE RIDGE (WEST FORT)

On June 14, Ewell ordered Early's division to strike West Fort, the smallest of the Union defenses around Winchester (directly in front of you from the Civil War Trails marker). General Milroy's third defensive work, West Fort was perhaps his most vulnerable. West Fort consisted of a series of unfinished lunettes nearly one-half mile west of Star Fort. It was open to the rear and could only hold elements of two infantry regiments and six guns. By late afternoon, Early's men, after a grueling flank march, arrived in this position and prepared to attack the fort. Within the hour, Early had his artillery pieces in position and by 6:00 p.m. ordered them to fire. Early's guns poured a destructive barrage of shells into the Federal position for nearly 45 minutes.

When the Confederate artillery fire slackened, the Louisiana Tigers of Hays's brigade launched their assault on the fort. Confederate infantrymen met little resistance during their advance through several orchards. The light resistance they did encounter came primarily from two Ohio regiments and a six-gun battery of Union artillery. Once near the base of West Fort, however, Federal soldiers released their long-held fire. It staggered Hays's men. Reorganized after the initial shock of the Federal fire, the Louisianans stormed the fort and captured it.

Return to Route 522 (North Frederick Pike) and make a right.

Travel 1.5 miles and make a left onto Fortress Drive. You will see signage for Star Fort on your left off of Fortress Drive. Star Fort was preserved and now maintained by the Shenandoah Valley Battlefields Foundation. There is a short interpretive trail inside the fort.

GPS: N 39 °.206634 W 78 °.164574

STOP 15: SECOND BATTLE OF WINCHESTER: STAR FORT

Milroy's position included a series of varying levels of earthworks and forts around the town of Winchester in the west and north. Additionally, numerous commanding heights ringed the area. The best-constructed of these works was Fort Milroy, also called Flag Fort. In June 1863, Fort Milroy could hold 2,200 men, supported by four 20-pound Parrott rifles and two 24-pound howitzers. To the north was Star Fort, approximately one mile north of Fort Milroy. Star Fort was smaller in size, but was still able to hold 300 to 400 men and eight guns. Star Fort's history stretched back to the early part of the war when, in 1861, it was merely a series of gun emplacements known as "Fort Alabama." It was not until Milroy's occupation of Winchester that this prepared position was strengthened into what the Confederate infantry saw in June 1863.

Defending Star Fort on June 14, 1863, were soldiers from Col. Andrew McReynolds's brigade and numerous pieces of artillery from Capt. Frederic W. Alexander's Baltimore Light Artillery. Initial contact with Confederates at Star Fort came from afar. When Hays's Tigers captured West Fort, Alexander's artillery unleashed a devastating fire on the Confederates in their captured prize. The fire was so intense inside West Fort that on several occasions Confederate troops pulled out of the fort itself and huddled on its reverse sides for protection. Only darkness brought an end to the firing on West Fort.

Sometime around 9:00 p.m. on June 14, Milroy held a council

A modern picture from inside Star Fort, which was preserved and restored by the Shenandoah Valley Battlefields Foundation. (dw)

of war with his other commanding officers and decided to retreat from Winchester. By 3:00 a.m., Ewell accomplished his objective: Milroy had abandoned Winchester and was on the move.

Return to Route 522 (North Frederick Pike) and make a right. (If you wish to visit downtown Winchester, which is the home to several museums and a historic district, make a left.) The tour will take you to the Stephenson's Depot Battlefield. After making a right onto Route 522, continue 0.8 miles and make a right onto Route 37 north/west. Travel for 3.9 miles (Route 37 will become Route 11 north). After 3.9 miles, make a right onto Route 761 (Old Charles Town Road). In 0.4 miles, make a right onto Route 662 (Milburn Road). The Civil War Trails markers will be on your right.

GPS: N 39 °.229753 W 78 °.109939

STOP 16: STEPHENSON'S DEPOT: ACTION AT THE BRIDGE

During the late hours of June 14, Ewell feared that the Federals might pull out of Winchester and an opportunity to crush Milroy would be lost. Ewell ordered Johnson's division north from Winchester to Stephenson's Depot to cut off any potential Union retreat along this route.

In the predawn hours, Johnson's division reached the Charles Town Road Bridge over the Winchester and Potomac Railroad southeast of the Martinsburg Turnpike. The pike provided an escape route north to Martinsburg, while the Charles Town Road led northeast to Charles Town. It was an excellent position to block both escape routes and enfilade the Union column while it marched.

While Johnson further developed his position with Brig. Gen. George Steuart's and Col. Jesse Williams's brigades, he sent forward some skirmishers that soon opened fire on the head of the Federal column. "I had gone but a short distance when I distinctly heard the neighing of horses and the sound of men moving . . ." Johnson reported later. "I had opportunely struck the head of the enemy's retreating column." Soon, the lead Federal units on the march left the turnpike and pushed southward towards the Confederate position. Regiments of Ohio soldiers made desperate attacks, but they were not enough to take the Confederate line, despite inflicting serious casualties among Steuart's Virginians.

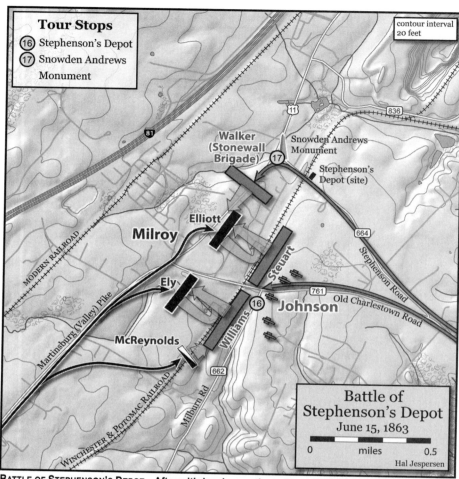

Tour Stops

(16) Stephenson's Depot
(17) Snowden Andrews Monument

contour interval 20 feet

Walker (Stonewall Brigade)
Snowden Andrews Monument
(17)
Stephenson's Depot (site)
Elliott
Milroy
Ely
Johnson
Old Charlestown Road
McReynolds
Steuart
Williams
Stephenson Road
MODERN RAILROAD
Martinsburg (Valley) Pike
Milburn Rd
WINCHESTER & POTOMAC RAILROAD

Battle of Stephenson's Depot
June 15, 1863

0   miles   0.5
Hal Jespersen

BATTLE OF STEPHENSON'S DEPOT—After withdrawing northward from Winchester, Milroy soon found himself nearly surrounded and annihilated by the hard-marching Confederates. The Shenandoah Valley was now clear for the Army of Northern Virginia to move northward.

Both armies fed reinforcements into the fight. Federal regiments continued to push their attacks toward the bridge over the railroad in order to clear the Confederate infantry out of their position. The numerous attempts took a toll on the Confederate gunners of Col. Snowden Andrews's artillery who were placed on the bridge itself. This was Andrews's first campaign back in command following a grievous wound that nearly killed him at the August 9, 1862, battle of Cedar Mountain. Lieutenant Randolph McKim, a nearby staff officer, joined in the defense of the guns and their vital position. "It was the key to our position," wrote McKim. "Lt. C.S. Contee was in command. His men fell around him till all were killed or wounded but himself and one other. . . . Unsupported except by a line of bayonets in the railway cut. . . . At every discharge the recoil carried the gun almost over the side of the bridge. . . . 2 sets of cannoneers, 13 out of 16 were killed or disabled." Of the fight for the guns at the bridge, General Lee in his report wrote that it was "the Thermopylae of my campaign."

After repeated assaults against the Confederate position along the railroad line and against the bridge over it, Milroy ordered his units to break off the attacks. As one historian of the battle wrote, "The victory was complete. With two brigades and eight guns, Johnson had routed Milroy. He had lost only 14 killed and 74 wounded. In addition to 3500 prisoners, Johnson captured 11 stands of colors, 175 horses, and arms and accoutrements [*sic*] of every description." Milroy escaped, but about half of his men did not. Coupled with this fight and fights at Winchester, Early's and Johnson's divisions of Ewell's Corps captured 23 cannons, 300 wagons brimming with supplies, and numerous other necessities for the Confederacy and the Army of Northern Virginia. Ewell's Corps continued to successfully clear out the Valley of Federal forces per Lee's objectives for the campaign, clearing the roads to Pennsylvania of Federal interference for the rest of their march.

Return to Route 761 (Old Charles Town Road) and make a left then a right onto Route 11 (Martinsburg Pike). Travel 0.6 miles and take a right onto Route 664 (Stephenson Road). The Snowden Andrews-Stephenson's Depot Monument will be on your immediate right.

GPS: N 39 °.238695 W 78 °.108340

STOP 17: STEPHENSON'S DEPOT: SNOWDEN ANDREWS MONUMENT

Dedicated on December 4, 1920, the Snowden Andrews Monument was erected in honor of Lt. Col. Richard Snowden Andrews. Commissioned by the family, the monument memorialized the work Andrews and his artillery did during the battle of Stephenson's Depot while his artillery battalion supported the center of Johnson's line.

Return to Route 11 (Martinsburg Pike) and make a

A monument to Snowden Andrews and his command's work during the battle of Stephenson's Depot was commissioned by his family and dedicated on December 4, 1920. (dw)

A modern day view of the bridge over the railroad where significant Union assaults were thrown back by artillery under Snowden Andrews. (dw)

right. You will now be following the general route of Early's and Johnson's divisions of Ewell's Corps. Rodes's division was in advance and, at the time of the Second Battle of Winchester, was already crossing the Potomac River at Williamsport, Maryland. Later in June, Hill's and Longstreet's Corps moved down the Shenandoah Valley east of Winchester and crossed various fords between Williamsport and Shepherdstown.

Travel on Route 11 for 1.4 miles and take a left onto Route 672 (Hopewell Road) then take Interstate 81 north. Travel Interstate 81 for 14.3 miles and take exit 12 onto Route 45 east. In 0.8 miles, take the right ramp for Route 45 and, at the end of the exit, make the left to remain on Route 45 (Queen Street). Remain on Queen Street for 1.2 miles and, at the intersection with King Street, the Civil War Trails marker is on your right in the median.

GPS: N 39°.456158 W 77°.963545

STOP 18: MARTINSBURG

As events unfolded in Winchester on June 14, 1863, Confederate infantry under Rodes and Confederate cavalry under Jenkins neared Martinsburg (in modern day West Virginia) from Berryville. Also headed to Martinsburg was Federal Brig. Gen. Daniel Tyler. Major General Robert Schenck of the Federal VIII Corps sent Tyler to Martinsburg to take over command of the Third Brigade, First Division, presently commanded by Col. Benjamin Smith. In all, Tyler had approximately 1,200 Union soldiers under his command "to support and cover the retreat of Maj. Gen. Robert H. Milroy from Winchester to Harpers Ferry." His force consisted of infantry from Ohio and New York and cavalry from Maryland, New York, and Pennsylvania. Tyler also had limited artillery in his force. Upon his arrival at the Baltimore and Ohio Railroad station, Tyler decided not to take command of these men as ordered; rather, he served as an extra officer on the field with whom tactical and strategic ideas could be discussed.

Meanwhile, Smith made a defense southeast of the town on Union Hill with his infantry and artillery. When Jenkins's cavalry arrived, Jenkins sent a message to Smith asking for his surrender in order to spare the town of shelling (despite the fact Jenkins had no artillery). Smith demurred and Jenkins, with not

Richard Snowden Andrews, a native of Maryland, raised the First Maryland Light Artillery early during the war. He received his first war wound during the Seven Days battles. On August 9, 1862, at Cedar Mountain, a second wound nearly disemboweled him, leaving Andrews out of the Confederate war effort for eight months. The battles at Second Winchester and Stephenson's Depot marked his first time back in the field and in command. (rsam)

enough of a force of his own, had to wait for Rodes to arrive with his infantry. In the meantime, Federal wagons laden with supplies used the Martinsburg-Williamsport Turnpike north of town unmolested and made their way safely into Pennsylvania.

By late afternoon on June 14, Rodes's 8,000-man infantry division arrived. Rodes's artillery deployed and immediately shelled the Federal position on Union Hill. Smith, aware that the Federal wagons cleared Martinsburg, felt he accomplished his mission and ordered a withdrawal. Despite some confusion, a majority of the Union command at Martinsburg got away, minus five pieces of artillery.

Return to Queen Street and continue on it north for 1.5 miles and make a right onto Route 11 (Williamsport Pike). Drive north on Route 11, and in 11.5 miles you will cross the Potomac River. The modern bridge is very close to the wartime ford used by Ewell's Confederates. As you cross the river into Williamsport, the road bears left. After this, take your first left into the C&O Canal National Park. Here there is a visitor center, restrooms, and access to the C&O Canal. The Civil War Trails marker is located on the towpath facing the Potomac River.

GPS: N 39 °.600974 W 77 °.826831

STOP 19: WILLIAMSPORT

On the evening of June 15, Confederates under Rodes and Jenkins crossed the Potomac River here at Williamsport. Rodes's mission was to clear any Federal resistance in the area, destroy the C&O Canal, and collect supplies. Jenkins rode northward to Chambersburg to capture supplies there. Rodes's men had marched twenty miles from Martinsburg to reach the Potomac. The men of the 14th North Carolina Infantry were given the honor to be the first Confederate foot soldiers to enter Maryland.

On June 18, Ewell arrived in Williamsport and ordered Rodes to move to Hagerstown. The goal was to threaten the Federal garrison at Harpers Ferry, though Lee did not have time to lay siege to the town as he had Jackson do in 1862. Lee knew by this point that Hooker was aware of his movement north and that time was of the essence. Soon, the fords between here and Shepherdstown witnessed nearly 75,000 Confederates crossing the Potomac.

After lackluster performances at both First Manassas in 1861 and Harpers Ferry in 1862, Brig. Gen. Daniel Tyler returned to command in the summer of 1863 and held several more posts in the Union army before resigning at the age of 65 in 1864. (loc)

Maj. Gen. Robert Schenck, a politically appointed general by President Lincoln, had served at First and Second Manassas and in the 1862 Valley Campaign. Not long after the Gettysburg campaign, he returned to politics and Congress. (loc)

An old army officer, Col. Benjamin F. Smith had seen service in the American West before the outbreak of the Civil War. Smith was promoted to colonel and placed in command of the 126th Ohio Volunteer Infantry in September 1862, a post he held during the Gettysburg campaign. (loc)

Turn left out of the C&O Canal parking lot onto West Potomac Street. In 0.4 miles, turn left onto Route 63 (North Artizan Street) and travel 3.2 miles. The Civil War Trails marker is on the right side of the road, opposite the intersection for McGregor Drive.

GPS: N 39 °.643896 W 77 °.803775

STOP 20: SHIELDING THE ARMY

By June 25, most of Lee's army was now north of the Potomac River and spread out in the Cumberland Valley west of South Mountain. Lee used the South Mountain range to screen his infantry from Hooker's scouts east of the mountains. The majority of Lee's cavalry was with Jeb Stuart in central Maryland, so Lee's infantry only had limited cavalry with it to scout and screen its movements. As Lee's men marched northward, Confederates wrote about the lush countryside as compared to the stripped-bare Virginia farmsteads: "All the country through which we passed today is beautiful and rich, splendid wheat, hay and corn crops," wrote Robin Berkeley of the Amherst (VA) Artillery.

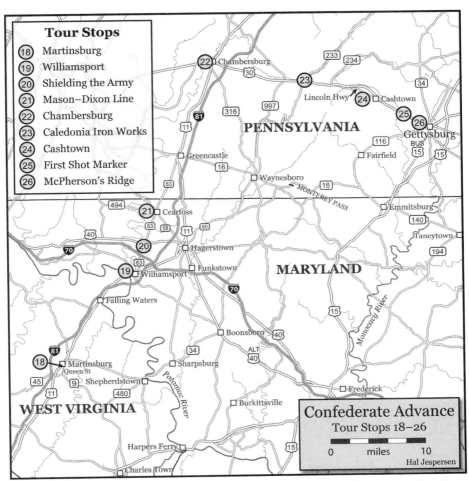

CONFEDERATE ADVANCE—Moving northward into Maryland and Pennsylvania, the Army of Northern Virginia used the mountains as a shield between them and the Army of the Potomac. Soon, Lee's army was stretched out across south-central Pennsylvania, with little knowledge of the Federal army's location.

Also by now, local residents began to flee the oncoming Confederate army. Later, few of them claimed any intrusions on private property—Lee had forbidden it in General Orders 72—but at the time, many did not want to take a chance. Confederate quartermasters issued Confederate script for most of the stores troops did take, but it was of little use to local citizens. Farmers fled the area north and east, as did the African American residents, fearful of capture and forced enslavement.

Continue north on Route 63 (Greencastle Pike) for 4.2 miles and enter into the village of Cearfoss. Make a left into the parking lot for a convenience store at the corner of Route 63 and Route 494. Two Civil War Trails markers are located in the parking lot facing Route 494.

GPS: N 39 °.699998 W 77 °.777087

STOP 21: CROSSING THE MASON AND DIXON

In this area, Rodes's Division first crossed into Pennsylvania on June 22. In the next few days, Hill's Corps and some of Longstreet's Corps followed. This moment was not lost on the men who wrote about "repaying" the northerners for the damage the southern farms and homes endured during the war. Many were proud to take the war to the people of the North— especially into Pennsylvania for the first time. Each division commander of Ewell's Corps was instructed to take public property only and pay for it in Confederate script. At many towns, the Confederates found that public warehouses had been emptied before their arrival.

As Lee's men raced towards Chambersburg and points north, local governments mobilized to protect the region. On June 15, President Lincoln issued a proclamation calling for 100,000 militiamen to turn out to confront the Confederate invasion: "I now appeal to all the citizens of Pennsylvania who love liberty and are mindful of the history and traditions of their revolutionary fathers," he wrote, "and who feel that it is a sacred duty to guard and maintain the free institutions of our country, who hate treason and its abettors, and who are willing to defend their homes and their firesides. . . ."

Return to Route 63 north (Greencastle Pike) and drive north. In 1.5 miles, you will cross the Mason Dixon Line into Pennsylvania. Continue for 4.7 miles, then take a left onto Route 11 (South Antrim Way). Travel for 11 miles on Route 11 into downtown Chambersburg. Due to one-way streets, take a right onto East Garfield Street, then a left onto South 2nd Street. In 0.8 miles, take a left onto Route 30 (Lincoln Highway); this will take you to the center of town. There are several historic markers around the traffic circle that relate to the town's Civil War history. There is also a walking tour of Civil War buildings that survived the burning in 1864. Of note is the Franklin County Courthouse.

GPS: N 39 °.937469 W 77 °.661292

STOP 22: CHAMBERSBURG

Late on June 14, after the affair at Martinsburg, Jenkins received orders to make his way to Chambersburg, Pennsylvania. The following day, June 15, the gray horsemen made their way into Pennsylvania, and twenty-four hours later, Jenkins's men reached their objective. This movement further secured Lee's line of march onto northern soil. Jenkins and his command worked to secure the town throughout June 16, both in presence and purchases with Confederate currency. Between June 15-17, Jenkins's troopers raided Chambersburg and the surrounding fields and farms, taking many foodstuffs for men and beast as well as other material the Confederate army desperately needed.

Chambersburg did not see the last of the Confederate army after the departure of Jenkins's troopers on June 17. One week later, Jenkins led the advance elements of the main body of the Army of Northern Virginia into Chambersburg and its surrounding environs. Between June 22 and 24, the Confederate Second Corps arrived. On June 26, Lee arrived just after Hill's Corps and established his headquarters east of town in Messersmith's Woods on the road to Gettysburg.

To continue on to Tour Stop 23 (Caledonia Iron Works, see page 41), take Route 11 (South Main Street) from the center of town one block and then make a left onto Lincoln Highway. After 0.6 miles, bear right on Route 30 east (Lincoln Highway) and travel 10 miles farther east. From Route 30 (Lincoln Highway) make a left onto Route 233 and then your immediate right into the Caledonia State Park parking lot. You will see the remains of the ironworks and interpretive markers.

Today a circa 1920's half scale reconstructed furnace stack is all that remains of the Caledonia Furnace and Iron Works. Here on June 26, Confederates under Jubal Early burned the iron works as "retaliation" for damages inflicted on the southern people. (cm)

Today, Chambersburg recognizes its own rich Civil War history with a memorial fountain and statue in the town square. A variety of historic signs can be found along the square's sidewalks. (cm)

Many historical markers, like this one, are located in the Chambersburg "Diamond." The markers cover not only the role of the town in the Gettysburg campaign but also the burning of Chambersburg by Confederates on July 30, 1864. (cm)

GPS: N 39 °.906732 W 77 °.477984—Caledonia State Park (Tour Stop 23)

If you wish to take the "Ewell's Invasion Alternate Tour Route," take South Main Street Route 11 (South Main Street) from downtown Chambersburg one block and make a left onto Lincoln Highway. After 0.6 miles, stay right onto Route 30 east (Lincoln Highway). In 1 mile, turn left to take the exit for Interstate 81 north. Stay on Interstate 81 north for 30.5 miles, then take Exit 47, Route 34 (Hanover Street). At the end of the exit, take a left onto Route 34 (Hanover Street). After 1 mile, turn left onto West High Street then make your next right onto North Pitt Street. The Cumberland County Historical Society is located at 21 North Pitt Street. The historical society has a museum and store that relates to local history and Civil War history. There are several Civil War-related interpretive markers around the historical society's side entrance at 37 West High Street, Carlisle, Pennsylvania 17013 (near the Cumberland Valley Visitors Center).

GPS: N 40 °.201738 W 77 °.191006—Civil War markers near Cumberland County Historical Society

ALTERNATE TOUR ROUTE: EWELL'S INVASION

After it entered Pennsylvania, the vanguard of the Army of Northern Virginia, the Confederate Second Corps, did not remain idle for long. By June 25, Ewell ordered two of his divisions, Rodes's and Johnson's, to march for Carlisle, Pennsylvania, site of an army barracks familiar to many officers in the Confederate army. Between 1838 and 1861, the army barracks in Carlisle served as a cavalry school for United States Army, and many former US officers, now fighting for the Confederacy, had been stationed here. Meanwhile, Early was ordered to head east towards Gettysburg, York, and beyond. Lee wrote to Ewell, "if Harrisburg comes within your means, capture it." Over the next several days, Ewell's command, along with Jenkins's cavalry, moved towards Carlisle but also Harrisburg. Events south of Harrisburg eventually forced Ewell to march south to rejoin Lee. But Ewell's forces made the farthest northern advance of the Army of Northern Virginia during the war.

GPS: N 40 °.201738 W 77 °.191006 – Civil War markers near Cumberland County Historical Society

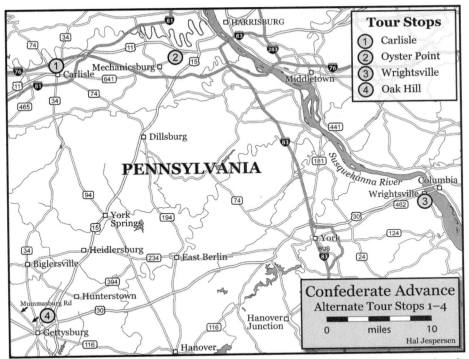

CONFEDERATE ADVANCE—Because the Confederate Second Corps was the first to invade Pennsylvania, it was tasked with threatening central Pennsylvania and the state capital of Harrisburg. Their marching columns created much panic and fear in state and federal officials.

ALTERNATIVE TOUR STOP 1: EWELL'S INVASION: CARLISLE

During June 27, Carlisle, Pennsylvania, hosted large portions of the Confederate Second Corps. In addition to Johnson's and Rodes's divisions, Jenkins's cavalry brigade arrived. The cavalrymen did not stay long, though; Ewell ordered them to screen the approaches to Harrisburg, the capital of Pennsylvania.

With two-thirds of the Second Corps on the march towards Harrisburg, Ewell's last division, under Early, continued east toward York.

While in Carlisle, Ewell obtained $50,000 worth of medicines, uniforms, arms, saddles, bridles, and foodstuffs—enough to feed two of his divisions. He sent the remainder back to Virginia. Treating the civilian population more gently than the property at Stevens's Iron Works, Ewell allowed clergy to hold their regular services, took "exceptional care" of Dickinson College, and did not burn the Carlisle Barracks, a strategic military

A 1860 view of a Market Day at the Hanover Street entrance to Carlisle, Pennsylvania. The Confederate occupation of Carlisle during the Gettysburg campaign did not last long. (loc)

installation. A few days later on July 1, Confederate Maj. Gen. Jeb Stuart's cavalry arrived in Carlisle looking for Ewell's infantry. He received orders here on the morning of July 2 to go to Gettysburg.

Just north of Carlisle is Sterrett's Gap. According to tradition, this gap in the Blue Mountains is the farthest northern advance of any troops of the Army of Northern Virginia. There is a small monument located on the side of the highway in the gap. Though not part of the driving tour, the GPS location is given below for those interested in visiting the monument. The monument is located in the front yard of a private home, and there is little room to pull over on the narrow, winding road, so please exercise extreme caution.

GPS: N 40 °.29534 W 77 °.13325–Sterrett's Gap Monument

From Carlisle, take High Street east approximately 3 miles and take the right exit for Interstate 81 north. Travel for 10.4 miles to Exit 59, Route 581 east. Once on Route 581 east, travel 5.1 miles (along the way, Route 581 east and Route 11 north share the same road). After 5.1 miles, take Exit 5, Route 15 north (South 32nd Street). In 0.5 miles, make a right onto Market Street and travel another 0.5 miles. Willow Park will be on your left. Take a left onto 24th Street, and the Civil War interpretive marker will be on your left in Willow Park. There are several other Civil War interpretive markers in Camp Hill. For more information, contact the Camp Curtin Historical Society at www.campcurtin.org.

GPS: N 40 °.241864 W 76 °.925081–Oyster Point

ALTERNATE TOUR STOP 2: EWELL'S INVASION: OYSTER POINT AND FORT COUCH

Also closing in on Harrisburg were Jenkins's troopers. Reaching Mechanicsburg around 9:00 a.m. on June 28, they began to encounter New York militia under the command of Brig. Gen. Joseph F. Knipe. Following a brief skirmish, Jenkins's men occupied the town and demanded that civic leaders provide food for his troopers. After their meals, Jenkins's command pushed four miles farther to the south and west of Harrisburg, where artillery riding with Jenkins traded shots with Union artillery defending the approaches to the Pennsylvania capital. Darkness brought an end to the artillery duel, and the Confederates returned to Mechanicsburg.

The following day, June 29, Jenkins and his men returned to Peace Church near Oyster Point but did not press Knipe's position initially. Instead, Ewell ordered a reconnaissance of the approaches to Harrisburg. Further actions, however, were in the future for Jenkins's men.

During the morning, following the reconnaissance, Ewell received a message from Lee for his command to return to the army and the concentration point at Chambersburg. Even as Ewell started to put the necessary orders in place, a portion of Jenkins's command charged the Union position at Oyster Point. When they reached the Union line, their attacked stalled due to a barricade blocking their path. Stymied, the cavalry was forced to withdraw, leaving behind a piece of artillery near the Oyster Point Hotel. It was not recovered until later in the day.

Further skirmishes occurred in the area as Ewell's and Jenkins's command headed south. "While this skirmish was of no particular account in itself, it is really historic," a veteran of the 22nd New York Regiment wrote of these brief encounters. "It was at the furthest northern point which was reached by the invaders, and marks the crest of the wave of the invasion of Pennsylvania." Soon Lee would change his orders and have Ewell concentrate on Gettysburg.

To visit the site of Fort Couch (built in June 1863 to defend Harrisburg from Confederate attack) return to Market Street and take a left. In 1.2 miles, turn left onto 9th Street. Travel 0.2 miles and make a right onto Ohio Avenue. The park is located at the corner of 8th Street and Ohio Avenue. Located here are portions of the fort, historic markers, and a monument to the Gettysburg campaign and Fort Couch.

GPS: N 40 °.246107 W 76 °.904182–Fort Couch

Also of note is the John Rupp House in nearby Mechanicsburg. Here, Brig. Gen. Albert Jenkins set up his headquarters June 28-30 awaiting the rest of Ewell's corps for a possible attack on Harrisburg. The house still stands with a monument to Jenkins next to the house. The Rupp House is located three miles from the Oyster Point Tour Stop.

GPS: N 40 ° .223843 W 76 °.975758–John Rupp House

From Willow Park, return to Market Street and make a left. In 0.6 miles, take a right onto South 17th Street. Travel 0.3 miles and

A Mexican War veteran, Brig. Gen. Joseph F. Knipe had seen action in the Valley Campaign in 1862 and at Cedar Mountain, Antietam, and Chancellorsville. During the Gettysburg campaign, he was recovering in Harrisburg, Pennsylvania, from a prior wound when his leadership on the field of battle became necessary again. (loc)

take a left onto Hummel Avenue. After 0.4 miles, make a right onto South 10th Street. In 0.5 miles, merge onto Interstate 83 south. Stay on Interstate 83 south for 19.8 miles to Exit 21, Route 30 east. Remain on Route 30 east for 10 miles and exit right onto Cool Springs Road south to Route 462. Take a right onto Route 462 (Hellam Street) and after 0.5 miles, take a left onto North 3rd Street. After four blocks, make a right onto Walnut Street. Follow Walnut Street all the way to where it dead-ends in a parking lot next to the Susquehanna River. There is a Civil War interpretive marker located near the end of the parking lot facing the river.

GPS: N 40 °.028515 W 76 °.529126

Also nearby, at the modern bridge location, is the Burning of the Bridge Diorama Museum. The museum is open seasonally and has a narrated diorama of the events on June 28, 1863.

GPS: N 40 °.025939 W 76 °.529216–Burning Bridge Diorama Museum

ALTERNATE TOUR STOP 3: EWELL'S INVASION: WRIGHTSVILLE

The Confederate army did not demonstrate nearly the same level of movement and activity on June 28 as it had the previous week. Lee's army was in constant motion for days and covered numerous miles against a backdrop of heat, humidity, and dry and dusty roads. For large portions of the army, then, rest was the order of the day.

A few elements of Ewell's corps, however, continued their move towards the Pennsylvania capital. Early's division marched to York, captured the town without opposition before placing a requisition and ransom on the citizens. Meanwhile, Gordon's brigade continued its advance to Wrightsville to capture and secure a covered bridge that connected with the town of Columbia, Pennsylvania, across the Susquehanna River. Once secured, Gordon's men would await the arrival of the rest of Early's division before moving to Lancaster and, eventually, Harrisburg from the rear.

Late on the afternoon of June 28, Gordon's brigade arrived in Wrightsville where they encountered militia. Gordon deployed his artillery and started to shell the Union defenders. Those soldiers were under the direct command of Col. Jacob Frick. In all, the ragtag command had nearly 1,300 soldiers compared to Gordon's 2,000 veterans. Colonel Frick's U-shaped defense was not enough to repel Gordon's grizzled veterans, and the line gave way. Federal soldiers made their way toward the bridge and across the span. During their retreat, the Federals set fire to the bridge after a failed detonation of one of its spans. Unfortunately, the fire grew in size and spread into the town of Wrightsville itself. Early's report of the campaign recorded that "[t]he bridge was entirely consumed, but the further progress of the flames was arrested by the exertions of Gordon's men." The burned bridge's stone piers remain standing in the river today.

Retrace your route down Walnut Street two blocks and make a left onto North 3rd Street, then your second right onto Locust Street. Take Locust Street west 0.5 miles (you will pass the Historic Wrightsville Museum on the left) and make a right onto North 9th Street (Cool Springs Road). After 0.7 miles, take the exit for Route 30 west. Travel 39.7 miles (through York, Thomasville, and New Oxford). Route 30 will take you into downtown Gettysburg. Take a right onto York Street. In two blocks, you will reach the town square. Take the first exit off the traffic circle onto Carlisle Street. Travel 0.4 miles on Carlisle Street and make a left onto West Lincoln Avenue. After two blocks, make a right onto College Avenue (which will turn into Mummasburg Road). After turning on College Avenue, travel 0.9 miles and make a right onto Confederate Avenue. The Peace Light Memorial will be in front of you.

A *Harpers Weekly* engraving of the burning of Wrightsville bridge during the Gettysburg campaign. (loc)

GPS: N 39 °.847810 W 77 °.243429

ALTERNATE TOUR STOP 4: GETTYSBURG NATIONAL MILITARY PARK: PEACE LIGHT MEMORIAL AT OAK HILL

The following day, June 29, Ewell received orders to march on Harrisburg. Despite Jenkins command making the necessary reconnaissance, a precursor to Ewell's march on the Pennsylvania capital, the order would never be carried out. When Lee learned of the proximity of the Army of the Potomac to his army, he quickly sent orders to his various far-flung commands to concentrate the army and prepare for a fight. Johnson's division got on the march first, ending their time on the road near Shippensburg that evening.

The other two divisions started moving towards

the concentration point the following day, June 30. At day's end, Rodes's division had reached Heidlersburg, while Early's division, also heading for Heidlersburg, camped within three miles of that destination. Johnson's division also marched on June 30, camping for the night at Scotland, halfway between Shippensburg to the north and Chambersburg to the south. As the battle of Gettysburg began the following day, July 1, Ewell's corps was yet again on the march. While more defined battle lines developed west of Gettysburg, two of Ewell's divisions, Rodes's and Early's, headed towards the right flank and rear of the Union line. Their approach to Gettysburg would be from the north and northeast.

Although the western approach to the town of Gettysburg contains many north-south ridges, perfect for military use, there is only one significant hill in this area in which the battle developed during the morning of July 1, 1863. Known locally as Oak Hill, it became a desired location for both Union and Confederate forces as the fighting grew in size. Major General Oliver Otis Howard, in command of all Federal forces on the field following the death of Maj. Gen. John Reynolds, wanted to extend the Federal battle line north along Oak Ridge and atop Oak Hill. It was not to be.

Ewell's Corps was still on the march during the early morning hours of July 1 as combat between Confederate infantry and artillery and Union cavalry began the battle of Gettysburg. The corps pushed towards Cashtown and Gettysburg per Lee's orders to concentrate the army. By mid-morning, the first division of soldiers from the corps to reach the battlefield was that of General Rodes. His brigades quickly deployed along both the wooded and open terrain of Oak Hill and went into action against the Union I Corps along Oak Ridge. Ewell's Corps

The Peace Light Memorial, dedicated during the 75th Anniversary of the battle of Gettysburg, sits atop Oak Hill.
(dw)

continued to arrive in Gettysburg, extending his line of battle across the northern plain north of the town of Gettysburg. Here, his men fought with elements of the XI Corps during the afternoon.

This is the end of the alternate tour route "Ewell's Invasion." To obtain a tour brochure to the Gettysburg battlefield, visit the Gettysburg National Military Park Visitor Center at 1195 Baltimore Pike, Gettysburg, Pennsylvania 17325.

If you are interested, the "Retreat from Gettysburg" chapter begins at the nearby Seminary Ridge Museum located at 111 Seminary Ridge, Gettysburg, Pennsylvania 17325. To reach the Seminary Ridge Museum, turn left out of the Peace Light parking lot onto Confederate Avenue. At the intersection with Mummasburg Road, continue straight onto Doubleday Avenue. Doubleday Avenue will make a sharp right turn and become Wadsworth Avenue. Make your next left turn onto Reynolds Avenue. Take Reynolds Avenue to Route 30 (Chambersburg Road) and make a left at the stop light onto Route 30. Take Route 30 for 0.3 miles and make a right onto Seminary Ridge. The Seminary Ridge Museum will be on your left with parking on your right.

GPS: N 39.832103 W 77.244588—Seminary Ridge Museum, beginning of "Retreat from Gettysburg" tour.

STOP 23: CALEDONIA IRON WORKS

The Confederate Second Corps divided its column heading toward two different objectives. Generals Rodes's and Johnson's divisions marched towards Carlisle via Shippensburg while Early's column, following a deluge of rain, marched toward Gettysburg and York via the Chambersburg Pike. During his march, Early ordered the burning of the Caledonia Iron Works on June 26, 1863. The ironworks were owned by Pennsylvania Congressman and staunch abolitionist Thaddeus Stevens. "My reasons for giving the order were founded on the fact that the Federal troops had invariably burned such works in the South," wrote Early in 1886. "Moreover, in some speeches in congress, Mr. Stevens had exhibited a most vindictive spirit toward the people of the South, as he continued to do to the day of his death. This burning was simply in retaliation for various deeds of barbarity perpetrated by Federal troops in some of the Southern States."

Pennsylvania politician, lawyer, and businessman Thaddeus Stevens's pro-abolitionist beliefs made his iron works a target for Early's Confederates. (loc)

Turn left out of the parking area onto Route 30 east (Lincoln Highway). As you drive east toward Gettysburg, you will be following the route of Hill's Corps. Take Route 30 for 2.8 miles and make a right onto Old Route 30, also called Lincoln Highway. This road follows the original wartime road between Chambersburg and Gettysburg. After 3.9 miles, you will be in the village of Cashtown. Take a left into the parking area for the iconic Cashtown Inn. There will be a Civil War Trails marker in front of the inn.

GPS: N 39 °.884581 W 77 °.360179

STOP 24: CASHTOWN

On June 29, Lee made his first attempts to concentrate his entire army since their entrance into Pennsylvania. According to Lee, "on the night of the 28th, information was received from a scout that the Federal Army, having crossed the Potomac, was advancing northward, and that the head of the column reached the South Mountain." With this intelligence, Lee called off Ewell's approach to and investment in the Pennsylvania state capital at Harrisburg, instead ordering him to "join the army at Cashtown or Gettysburg." Lee also ordered his other two corps, Longstreet's and Hill's, to move towards the concentration point of the Cashtown-Gettysburg area. "Hill's corps was accordingly ordered to move toward Cashtown on the 29th, and Longstreet to follow the next day," Lee recorded in his January 1864 report of the campaign.

Throughout June 30, the Confederate army continued to march to the concentration area of Cashtown and Gettysburg. Generals Anderson's and Heth's divisions were in Cashtown by the end of the day while the last division of Hill's Corps, under Maj. Gen. Dorsey Pender, remained in camp at Fayetteville.

As darkness consumed the landscape that night of June 30, the Confederate army, though well concentrated, still had large geographic spaces to cover to finish the concentration before it could risk combat with the Federal army. That evening, Lee's Army of Northern

Modern image of the Cashtown Inn, a building that vast numbers of Confederate soldiers marched by at the end of June and beginning of July 1863. (dw)

Virginia had only four of its nine infantry divisions east of South Mountain. Although more of the army was near at hand, there was a distinct disadvantage because of the terrain. A majority of Lee's army was on the western side of South Mountain. If Lee needed to call upon more of his army the following day, its scattered elements would have to crowd onto a single road through the Cashtown Pass over steep inclines and cover a distance of 10 miles.

Turn left out of the parking area and continue east on Old Route 30 (Lincoln Highway). After 2.5 miles, you will continue straight onto modern Route 30 (Lincoln Highway). In 2.2 miles, you will reach the intersection of Route 30 and Knoxlyn Road. Just off the left side of Route 30 is the small "First Shot Marker." Please park cautiously and move alertly as there is not a dedicated parking area for this monument.

GPS: N 39 °.850917 W 77 °.280826

Maj. Gen. Dorsey Pender skyrocketed through the command structure of the Army of Northern Virginia. Pender was one of the youngest Confederate generals, promoted to the rank of major general at age 29. (usamhi)

STOP 25: FIRST SHOT MARKER

July 1, 1863, was not the first time enemy combatants fired a "first shot" at Gettysburg. While on the march eastward on June 26, Early "had heard on the road that there was probably a force at Gettysburg . . . ." With this information, Early ordered a force to Gettysburg; "the object of this movement was . . . to amuse and skirmish with the enemy while I [Early] should get on his flank and rear, so as to capture his whole force."

Writing from the safety of Harrisburg on June 29, Pvt. Henry Wirt Shriver of the 26th Pennsylvania Volunteer Militia recalled the initial clash with Confederate forces west of Gettysburg. "Such confusion I never saw," recalled Shriver. "[E]verybody gave orders and nobody obeyed— we were all green and knew nothing about regular forming, and half the right was skedaddling already." Once the militia was pushed aside and Early arrived at the head of the column nearing Gettysburg, the general entered the town itself and placed a requisition for supplies on the townspeople. Early and his column did not stay long. By the morning of June 27, they were back on the march. The column marched through Mummasburg, Hunterstown, New Chester, Hampton, and East Berlin, before they encamped a short distance beyond Berlin. The first Confederate attack and occupation of Gettysburg was over.

A monument on the Gettysburg battlefield honors the first shot of the battle, July 1, 1863. (dw)

Brig. Gen. John B. Gordon commanded a brigade of Georgians in the Army of Northern Virginia and was part of the Confederate force that marched on Gettysburg on June 26, 1863. (loc)

Several days later, "On July 1, at 5 a.m. Heth took up the line of march," wrote General Hill. With the failure of Pettigrew's brigade to capture stores and supplies in Gettysburg the previous day (see next stop), Heth's division was heading east down the Chambersburg Pike to continue where the North Carolinians had left off. By 7:30 a.m., the lead units were within several miles of the borough itself. Buford's cavalry, which had screened the approaches to Gettysburg since the evening prior, took notice. A young lieutenant, Marcellus Jones, checking on his vidette post on Wisler's Ridge along the Chambersburg Pike, spotted the column. Seeing a trooper nearby preparing to fire on the Confederate marchers more than 700 yards away, Jones, with no weapon of his own on hand, yelled, "Hold on, George, give me the honor of opening this ball." George handed Jones a cavalry carbine and, with the crack of that carbine, Jones fired the first shot of the battle of Gettysburg.

Continue east on Route 30 (Lincoln Highway) 1.8 miles and turn into the Gettysburg National Military Park West End Guide station on McPherson's Ridge.

GPS: N 39 °.837910 W 77 °.252374

STOP 26: MCPHERSON'S RIDGE

"On the morning of June 30, I ordered Brigadier-Gen. Pettigrew to take his brigade to Gettysburg, search the town for army supplies (shoes especially), and return the same day," wrote General Heth. And so one of the longest-enduring myths and fallacies of the Gettysburg campaign was born. No shoe factory existed in the town of 2,400 citizens, nor would the town have had much left to offer anyway. This is illustrative of the problems of Confederate communications during the campaign and then tactically during the battle: Heth and his superior, Hill, should have known that Early's division had already been through Gettysburg four days earlier and already acquired what few supplies had not been sent away by the townspeople.

Regardless of this enduring myth, Confederate forces were on the march down the Chambersburg Pike towards Gettysburg on June 30. As Pettigrew's command reached the north-south ridges west of Gettysburg, such as McPherson's Ridge, Pettigrew observed what he thought to be elements of the Army of the Potomac, particularly cavalry. According to all the information given to Pettigrew, the Federal army was miles away to the south, and he should encounter no resistance except militia or home guard units. "On reaching the suburbs of Gettysburg, Gen. Pettigrew," however, "found a large force of cavalry near the town, supported by an infantry force," wrote Heth in his official report. What happened next was far different from the report itself.

Pettigrew knew not to bring on a fight, and despite his years of service in the Confederate army, he was relatively green to brigade and field command. Nevertheless, Pettigrew made an important decision not to push the issue to gain entrance to Gettysburg. As Heth reported in September, "Under these circumstances, he did not deem it advisable to enter the town, and returned, as directed, to Cashtown." When Pettigrew arrived in Cashtown, he reported to both Heth and Hill that he believed that the force that blocked his way into Gettysburg was Federal cavalry from the Army of the Potomac. Both Heth and Hill on June 30 refused to believe Pettigrew's observations. Hill had been with Lee earlier and saw where Lee believed the Army of the Potomac to be: in the vicinity of Frederick, Maryland—certainly not Gettysburg. The young brigadier had merely seen home guard and militia. Because of Pettigrew's perceived failed mission, Heth asked Hill's permission to return to Gettysburg the following day, July 1, and accomplish what Pettigrew had not: a search of the town for supplies and the mythological cache of shoes. Hill gave permission—a fateful decision that influenced the next three days in American history.

This concludes the "Confederate Advance" route. To obtain a tour brochure to the Gettysburg battlefield, visit the Gettysburg National Military Park Visitor Center at 1195 Baltimore Pike, Gettysburg, Pennsylvania 17325. If you are interested, the "Retreat from Gettysburg" route tour begins at the nearby Seminary Ridge Museum located at 111 Seminary Ridge, Gettysburg, Pennsylvania 17325.

A Confederate divisional commander in Gen. Hill's Third Corps during the Gettysburg campaign, Maj. Gen. Henry Heth had served in several roles since the outbreak of the war. It was Heth's official report of the battle that started the Gettysburg "shoe" debate that still resonates in Gettysburg historiography today. (loc)

After being severely wounded at the battle of Seven Pines— and time as a Union prisoner of war—Brig. Gen. James Johnston Pettigrew returned to command his North Carolina brigade shortly before it was assigned to Gen. Lee and the Army of Northern Virginia for the Gettysburg campaign. (na)

The Union Response

CHAPTER TWO

This route will follow portions of the Left and Right Wing of the Army of the Potomac from Fredericksburg to Gettysburg. The entire route is approximately 150 miles in length.

While General Lee worked to carry out his plan, Maj. Gen. Joe Hooker pondered his next move following his defeat at Chancellorsville. The Union retreat returned the army to their old encampment north and east of Fredericksburg across the Rappahannock River. Once there, the recent reverses on the field were discussed at length among all levels of army personnel. Major General Oliver O. Howard, commander of the Union army's XI Corps, took a majority of the blame for the recent loss. His corps, positioned on the flank of the Union army during the battle, yielded to the devastating flank attack by Stonewall Jackson. General Howard wrote to his wife at the end of May that "everybody who is to blame tries to shift the responsibility upon somebody else's shoulders."

Hooker soon regained his confidence and started the process of resuming the offensive against Lee. However, not everyone believed this was the best course of action for the Army of the Potomac. On May 14, President Abraham Lincoln wrote to Hooker: "It does not now appear probable to me that you can gain anything by an early renewal of the attempt to cross the Rappahannock. I therefore shall not complain if you do no more for a time than to keep the enemy at bay, and out of other mischief by menaces and occasional cavalry raids, if practicable, and to put your own army in good condition again." Hooker accepted Lincoln's suggestion, and the

A modern image of the Monocacy Aquaduct. The structure, now part of a National Park, has not changed since the days of the Gettysburg campaign. (dw)

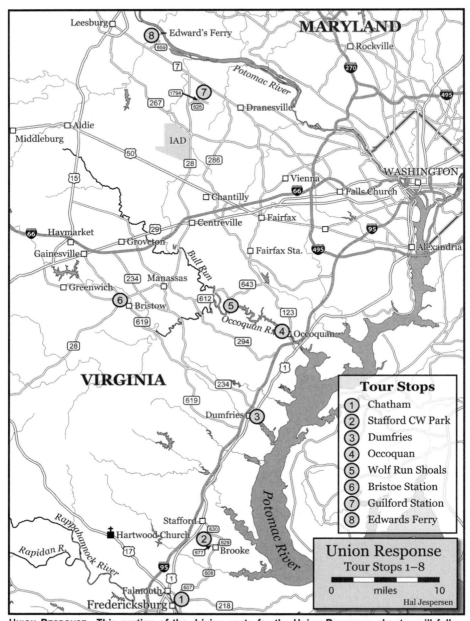

UNION RESPONSE—This portion of the driving route for the Union Response chapter will follow various corps of the Army of the Potomac from the positions around Fredericksburg in early June 1863 to the Potomac River.

Army of the Potomac remained quiet as they sought to rebuild.

While Hooker worked to restore his men and material, the Army of the Potomac faced the additional loss of thousands more men—troops who had joined

LEFT: An image of President Abraham Lincoln taken by war photographer Alexander Gardner just weeks after the end of Gettysburg campaign on August 9, 1863. (loc)

RIGHT: Maj. Gen. Oliver O. Howard, commander of the XI Corps, was derided for his corps's performance at Chancellorsville in May 1863. (loc)

the army in 1861 under two-year enlistments that were now about to expire. Furthermore, during the crisis summer of 1862, the army raised emergency troops under nine-month enlistments. All of these enlistments were set to expire during May and June. Gettysburg historian Edwin Coddington estimated that between April and June, 23,000 men left the ranks of the Union army. Coupled with the casualties from Chancellorsville, the Army of the Potomac lost nearly 32 percent of its total strength. The loss of these men, all battled-hardened veterans by this point, forced a reorganization of the army. Brigades were broken up and regiments reassigned to different divisions. Units that lost significant numbers of men from their terms of service were consolidated.

Federal cavalry was in far worse shape than the infantry. Between losses from the Chancellorsville campaign and the detachment of various units to other assignments, the effective number of cavalrymen in the Army of the Potomac dropped from 11,542 on April 30, to 4,677 by May 27, 1863—a

Company I, 6th Pennsylvania Cavalry, taken at Falmouth, Virginia at the beginning of the Gettysburg campaign in June 1863. This was just one of the many cavalry units Joe Hooker had to repair following the most recent campaign. (loc)

Hooker worked to reorganize the artillery in May 1863. This James Gibson image shows Batteries C & G, 3rd United States Artillery, in the field at Fair Oaks, Virginia, in June 1862. (loc)

60 percent loss. With regard to the Union artillery, Hooker felt he had too much, cutting the number of guns with the army by 10 percent and sending the excess back to army depots. Hooker also changed the way he assigned artillery, no longer dividing it up by division; rather, he grouped it into artillery brigades and then added those brigades to each corps. The artillery brigades consisted of five batteries, each with six guns per battery. Two other brigades of artillery were assigned to the Federal cavalry and another five to the Artillery Reserve. As with their Confederate counterparts, the reorganization increased artillery efficiency and the ability to concentrate fire more quickly during an engagement.

Resting, refitting, and reorganizing the Army of the Potomac during the month of May did little to prepare it for another campaign, particularly one of the scope that the Gettysburg campaign evolved into. The morale of the army was low and confidence in its leadership lower. The vast numbers of experienced soldiers leaving the ranks only furthered the problems that the army already faced. With the next campaign on the horizon, the state of the Army of the Potomac left much to be desired.

Begin the "Union Response" Chapter Tour at Historic Chatham located at 120 Chatham Lane, Fredericksburg, Virginia 22405. Chatham was used as a hospital after the battle of Chancellorsville. The Army of the Potomac was spread out in southern Stafford County. Today Chatham serves as a museum and headquarters for Fredericksburg and Spotsylvania National Military Park.

GPS: N 38° .309076 W 77° .454240

STOP 1: CHATHAM

With large portions of the Confederate army in motion June 3 and 4, 1863, intelligence reports came into army headquarters from all across the Federal line. The V Corps and VI Corps were positioned along the Rappahannock River. Some units were posted on the heights and manor property of Chatham, the home of Confederate officer James Lacy, opposite the town of Fredericksburg. Chatham once served as a Federal headquarters but now served as a hospital. The remainder of the army took supporting positions in the rear as far north as Stafford Court House, with Hooker's main headquarters near White Oak.

Some reports noted that large stretches of the Confederate works had been abandoned. Other reports recorded clouds of dust being kicked up from marching columns. In response, Hooker ordered Maj. Gen. John Sedgwick to make a reconnaissance in force across the Rappahannock River. Sedgwick selected the Vermont Brigade, Col. Lewis A. Grant commanding, as well as one New Jersey regiment, the 26th, to traverse the river in pontoon boats. The regiments did excellent work, capturing some 150 prisoners from Confederate Gen. A.P. Hill's Third Corps. Reacting to the probe, Hill sent Maj. Gen. William D. Pender's division eastward to the area of the VI Corps's crossing. The quick arrival thwarted any further efforts made by Sedgwick's men. General Lee, in a letter to President Davis on June 7, recorded the action: "After driving back our sharpshooters, under a furious cannonade from their batteries, by a force of skirmishers, they crossed a small body of troops, and occupied the back of the river."

Hooker kept Lincoln appraised of the situation along the Rappahannock and also shared his beliefs about Lee's intentions. Based on available intelligence, Hooker guessed that Lee was setting out on a campaign similar to the one of the previous summer. As he would not be able to steal a march on Lee, Hooker proposed to attack the rear element at Fredericksburg. Neither Lincoln nor General in Chief Henry Halleck liked Hooker's plan, though. Lincoln feared Hill's Corps at Fredericksburg was a trap. At the same time, the Confederate position was heavily fortified and would require a massive loss of life to successfully attack it. If Hooker proceeded with this plan, Lincoln wrote, he could become "entangled upon the river, like an ox jumped half over a fence and liable to be torn by dogs front and rear, without a fair chance to gore one way or kick the other." Hooker decided not to pursue this plan. The commanding general proposed yet another

Maj. Gen. Henry Halleck's early war successes led to his transfer from the Western Theater to Washington, D.C., where he became general-in-chief. The relationship between Halleck and Hooker during the Gettysburg campaign placed a strain on the Union high command. (loc)

Prewar teacher and lawyer Col. Lewis Grant joined the Union war effort in the fall of 1861. Wounded at Fredericksburg in December 1862, Grant recovered and returned to the army in time to command the famed Vermont brigade during the Chancellorsville campaign at the battle of Second Fredericksburg. (loc)

A modern image of Chatham, owned during the war by James Lacy. The house was used as a headquarters during the Fredericksburg campaign and then a hospital. Today, it is part of the Fredericksburg and Spotsylvania National Military Park. (cm)

plan not long after his first. This time, the Army of the Potomac would set upon a raid towards Richmond. Yet again, Lincoln and Halleck rejected Hooker's latest campaign ideas.

Exit out of the Chatham parking lot toward the right towards River Road. Make a left at River Road and then a left onto Route 3 (Kings Highway). As soon as you turn left onto Route 3, you will make your immediate left onto Route 212 (Chatham Heights Road) and travel 1 mile to the intersection with Route 218 (Butler/White Oak Road). Make a right onto Route 218, then take your immediate left onto Route 607 (Deacon Road).

If you continue east on Route 218 (White Oak Road), you will drive by the vicinity of General Hooker's headquarters. There is a state historic marker located just over a mile on Route 218. Also in 4.2 miles is the White Oak Civil War Museum.

After you turn onto Route 607 (Deacon Road), continue for 2.9 miles and make a left onto Route 608 (Brooke Road). Drive 4.7 miles and make a left onto Route 677 (Mt. Hope Church Road). In 1.2 miles, you will see the entrance to the Stafford Civil War Park on your left. There are self-guided walking trails that highlight the Federal encampments here in 1862-1863.

GPS: N 38 °.392265 W 77 °.401189

STOP 2: STAFFORD CIVIL WAR PARK

Stafford County hosted the majority of the Army of the Potomac from November 1862 through June 1863. The winter encampments of the XI and XII Corps were in this vicinity. After the battle of Chancellorsville, large portions of the Federal army returned to this area and their former camps around Falmouth. Some Federal units continued to mark time in this area as late as June 6 because Hooker was still unsure of Lee's plans.

First Corps commander, and later wing commander, Maj. Gen. John F. Reynolds. (loc)

At 3:00 p.m. that afternoon, Hooker wired Halleck that he was sending all of his cavalry and 3,000 infantry towards Culpeper Court House to further gather intelligence on Lee's intentions. The column was under the command of Brig. Gen. Alfred Pleasonton and was ordered to cross the Rappahannock not far from Brandy Station on the Orange and Alexandria Railroad. After crossing the river, Pleasonton was ordered to find the Rebel force reported to be at Culpeper and "disperse and destroy" those forces as well as any supplies and wagon trains. In all, 11,000 Union soldiers headed towards Lee's concentration point.

Two days later, June 8 passed by without any activity. It was not until late in the evening that the only Federal forces of the day moved out. Pleasonton moved his command up to the eastern bank of the Rappahannock with his troopers near both Beverly and Kelly's fords. With darkness blanketing the area, June 9 was destined to bring battle. Federals crossed the river in the early morning hours, triggering an engagement that lasted 14 hours. Brandy Station ended up as the largest cavalry battle during the American Civil War.

The results of the battle of Brandy Station caused Hooker to not only question Lee's intentions, but the movement of the Army of the Potomac. "If left to operate from my own judgment with my present information," Hooker wrote Lincoln, "I do not hesitate to say that I should adopt this course as being the most speedy and certain mode of giving the rebellion a mortal blow." Accordingly, only a small percentage of the Federal army, a majority of which was Pleasonton's command returning from the battle of the previous day, moved on June 10.

June 11 was to be a different day in the Army of the Potomac. Following the battle of Brandy Station, Hooker now believed that there was, in fact, Confederate infantry at Culpeper Court House. Because of his belief, Hooker sought, throughout June 11 and into June 12, to place his army in a position to counter this perceived Confederate threat. The shifting of the Union army that occurred over these two days now stretched the Army of the Potomac in a battle line of more than forty miles, from just south of Fredericksburg to Beverly Ford.

With an increased presence of Union forces on the far right, Hooker decided to shift the command responsibility of these several corps from his immediate oversight to someone actually on that front. Maj. Gen. John F. Reynolds was now responsible for the right wing of the Federal army—the I, III, V, XI, and Cavalry corps —the majority of the Army of the Potomac. This was similar to the Grand Divisions that the Army of the Potomac once used as an organizational command structure under Maj. Gen. Ambrose Burnside. Hooker then focused on the left wing and a possible withdrawal from the Fredericksburg front. Still unsure of Lee's intentions, Hooker wanted the left wing ready should he need to steal a quick march.

As information and intelligence continued to flood into Joe Hooker's headquarters, he finally became convinced that most of the Army of Northern Virginia was on the move and heading north and west. He reacted quickly by getting large portions of his army in motion.

Preserved defensive positions of the Army of the Potomac's XI Corps from their encampment in this area during the winter and spring of 1863. The steep embankment on the right side of the image illustrates just a small portion of these positions. (dw)

Leave the park and follow Deacon Road back to Route 608 (Brooke Road) and make a left. Drive 0.4 miles and make a left onto Route 629 (Andrew Chapel Road). Travel Route 629 for about 1 mile and make a left onto Route 630 (Courthouse Road). Stay on Route 630 for 3.3 miles (traveling through Stafford Courthouse). Take the right exit ramp for Interstate 95 north and continue on Interstate 95 north for 12 miles. Take Exit 152A to Route 234 south (Dumfries Road). Stay on Route 234 for 0.5 miles and make a right onto Route 1 south (Jefferson Davis Highway). After 0.6 miles turn right into a parking lot for Williams Ordinary. There is a Civil War Trails marker in the parking lot. Williams Ordinary is a large, brick building on the right (southbound) side of Route 1. The building is open occasionally and is the administrative offices for the Prince William County Historic Preservation Division. Williams Ordinary, built circa 1760, served as a hotel/tavern during the 19th century.

GPS: N 38 °.568877 W 77 °.323401

STOP 3: DUMFRIES

A long day of marches resumed on June 13 for the Federal army. In the west that day, the I, V, and XI Corps averaged marches of twenty to twenty-five miles. The pace was grueling, and for the V Corps, a driving rainstorm made it worse. These units continued to follow the Orange and Alexandria Railroad line as it angled northeastward towards northern Virginia. The right wing of the Federal army, under the watchful of eye of Hooker, also had a long day of campaigning on June 13. The VI Corps worked to remove the pontoon boats over the river to Fredericksburg before making their northward march, while the XII Corps led the line of march on the Telegraph Road towards Dumfries. The II Corps, meanwhile, was designated as the rear guard for this wing and waited until all of these Federal units had cleared the Falmouth area before beginning their march north.

At 7:00 p.m. that evening, Hooker wired Halleck in Washington, D.C., apprising him of the most current intelligence and how he planned to use it: "All my sources of information confirm the statement that Longstreet's and Ewell's corps have passed through Culpeper and Sperryville, toward the Valley. . . . [I]n view of this movement of the enemy

[I will] transfer the operations of this army from the line of the Aquia to the Orange and Alexandria Railroad." Hooker further informed his superiors that his orders and movements of the army would be further "governed by the movements of the enemy," with "the object being to bring the two wings together as far in advance on that line as the movements of the enemy will justify." Ending his communication, Hooker informed Halleck, "To-morrow p.m. my headquarters will be at Dumfries."

June 14, 1863, brought more arduous marches for the Army of the Potomac. Both wings were on the move early and covered vast distances of more than twenty to twenty-five miles. Some columns marched throughout the day and into the twilight hours. The Federal I and III Corps pushed on following the Orange and Alexandria Railroad, arriving in the vicinity of Catlett's Station south of Bristoe Station and Manassas Junction. The XI Corps had left that area that morning and had pushed north, through Bristoe and Manassas, ending their march just short of Centreville.

Hooker's wing of the army also trudged through the record-breaking June heat. The VI Corps continued to unite its commands near Stafford Court House, along the Telegraph Road, before moving north; meanwhile the II Corps broke camp but made little movement beyond that work. The XII

A period image of Catlett Station. Numerous soldiers from both sides went through this area, including the Union army during the Gettysburg campaign. (loc)

Corps, having just completed an all-night march and arriving at Dumfries at 9:00 a.m on June 14, rested beside Hooker's command headquarters. Nor did the II Corps move on June 14 as it was designated the rear guard. When these soldiers finally started their northward movement, General Hancock collected the stragglers and soldiers struck down from sunstroke as he went.

With his headquarters at Dumfries, Hooker communicated back and forth with Lincoln regarding the events in Winchester, Virginia. The president had a murky picture. "So far as we can make out here, the enemy have Milroy surrounded at Winchester and Tyler at Martinsburg," he wrote. "If they could

Alfred Waud sketched Dumfries, Virginia, during the Gettysburg campaign in June 1863. (loc)

hold out a few days, could you help them?" At the same time Lincoln looked to Hooker for the relief of Federal forces in the Valley, he told Hooker how he viewed the present strategic situation and hoped he could urge Hooker into further action. "If the head of Lee's army is at Martinsburg and the tail of it on the Plank Road between Fredericksburg and Chancellorsville, the animal must be very slim somewhere. Could you not break him?" Lincoln asked.

Four hours later Hooker responded, not addressing Lincoln's earlier concerns, but rather asking for further intelligence on the situation in the Valley: "Has anything further been heard from Winchester? I do not feel like making a move for an enemy until I am satisfied as to his whereabouts. To proceed to Winchester and have him [Confederate forces] make his appearance elsewhere, would subject me to ridicule," wrote Hooker. Furthermore, "With this feeling, unless otherwise directed . . . I will not. . . issue my order of march until the last moment, in the hope that further information may be received."

Turn left out of the parking lot onto Main Street. Main Street will bend back around to Route 1 north (Jefferson Davis Highway). Once you get to Route 1, turn left and travel for 0.6 miles and make a left onto Route 234 north (Dumfries Road). In 0.5 miles, take the right exit ramp for Interstate 95 north. Stay on Interstate 95 north for 7.4 miles and take exit 160B to Route 123 north. Travel Route 123 (Gordon Boulevard/ Ox Road) for 0.9 miles and take a left onto Commerce Street (into the town of Occoquan). In 0.1 miles, make a right onto Washington Street and travel two blocks to make a left onto Mill Street. At the end of Mill Street will be the Mill House Museum on your right, and a Civil War Trails marker facing the river (to the left of the museum).

GPS: N 38 °.685639 W 77 °.263314

STOP 4: OCCOQUAN

Since 1861, this area saw numerous river crossings by both Union and Confederate armies because of the several fords nearby. Now a large portion of Hooker's wing of the Army of the Potomac, the army's supply trains, and much of the hospital and supply stores were on the road north across the Occoquan on June 14. The pontoon bridge that Hooker built to cross the river was impressive. One Union soldier noted that the bridge was more than 300 feet in length, comprised of 121 pontoon boats.

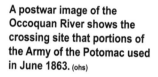

A postwar image of the Occoquan River shows the crossing site that portions of the Army of the Potomac used in June 1863. (ohs)

Over the next several days, Hooker and this wing of the Army of the Potomac continued to use the crossing at Occoquan. Patrick Taylor, a soldier in the 1st Minnesota Volunteer Infantry, wrote in his diary on June 16 that his

marching column "Left at 11 a.m. and at noon we hear that Harpers Ferry is infected by Lee. Crossed Occoquon [*sic*] River a half hour before sunset, camped and bathed. . . . The river is fordable here but the infantry crossed one channel on the bridge to a small island, and then forded the other channel."

Turn around and head back down Mill Street for 0.1 miles and make a right onto Union Street. In two blocks, make a left onto Commerce Street and follow Commerce Street back to Route 123 (Gordon Boulevard/Ox Road). Take a left onto Route 123 north and stay on Route 123 for 6.1 miles. Take a left onto Route 643 (Henderson Road) and continue for 2.5 miles and bear left to remain on Route 643. In 0.3 miles, take a left onto Wolf Run Shoals Road. Follow this road until it dead-ends into a parking lot for the Bull Run-Occoquan Trail. A Civil War Trails marker will be near the trailhead. There is also a trail that will partly follow the original road bed to the ford. The river was dammed between the 1930s and 1950s causing it to become much wider with the original ford crossing site 25 feet below water.

GPS: N 38 °.727916 W 77 °.358780

STOP 5: WOLF RUN SHOALS

Throughout the rest of the evening of June 15 and 16, Hooker continued to telegraph Lincoln with no reply. Large portions of the Federal army consolidated around Manassas Junction and Centreville and did not move on June 16. Only Hooker's wing, along the Telegraph Road, marched at all, the II Corps ending its march near Wolf Run Shoals and the VI Corps near Fairfax Court House.

Wolf Run Shoals was yet another Occoquan River crossing site the Army of the Potomac used during its march northward. The shoals was not far from the other crossing used by the Federal army in June 1863. Here at Wolf Run Shoals, the army's II and VI corps, as well as the Artillery Reserve, crossed the Occoquan. Eldridge B. Platt, an artillerist in the 2nd Connecticut Light Artillery Battery, not only recalled crossing the Occoquan River at Wolf Run Shoals, but also the hard marching during this period of the campaign (Platt's original spelling and grammar have been left intact): "I tell you we have seen a hard time sence we have left verginia we left Wolf run Shoals June 25th and have ben traveling most ever sence." When the last of the Federal units crossed at

Wolf Run Shoals, Gen. Hooker ordered the Second Vermont Brigade, which was guarding the fording site, to bring up the rear of the column and cross the river as well. When the Vermonters left the ford, it remained

unguarded and was later used by Jeb Stuart's Confederate horsemen during their daring ride around the Army of the Potomac.

Turn around and take Wolf Run Shoals Road back to make a left onto Route 643 (Henderson Road). Stay on Route 643 for 2.2 miles (Caution, the road has sharp curves and hills). Take a left onto Route 612 (Old Yates Ford) and continue for 3.2 miles. Make a right onto Route 294 (Prince William Parkway) and travel 1.8 miles, then take a left to remain on Route 294 (Prince William Parkway). Travel 2 miles and go straight at the light to take Brentsville Road. Starting at the intersection, travel 2.5 miles and make a left onto Lucasville Road, then your immediate right onto Route 619 (Bristow Road). Travel 4.1 miles (through Brentsville and Bristoe Station) and make a left onto Iron Brigade Unit Avenue. Bristoe Station Battlefield Heritage Park will be on your left at the traffic circle.

A modern view of the Wolf Run Shoals Road leading towards the crossing site. Confederate cavalry under Jeb Stuart would cross here as well on their way to Maryland. (dw)

GPS: N 38 °.727083 W 77 °.544172

STOP 6: BRISTOE STATION

At the end of the second week of the Gettysburg campaign, the Army of the Potomac spent a lot of time in northern Virginia and Prince William County. The river fords and crossing sites at Occoquan and Wolf Run Shoals both sit within the county, as does Dumfries, the site of Hooker's headquarters for two days during the campaign. Prince William County was no stranger to the war by 1863. The battles of First and Second Manassas had taken place on the same fields in the county in July 1861 and August 1862. Bristoe Station, just outside of Manassas, was also a witness to the hard hand of war. A year previously, a small battle was fought here as a precursor to Second Manassas. In the fall of 1863, the armies clashed in Bristoe yet again.

During this phase of the Gettysburg campaign, thousands of soldiers in the left wing of the Army of the Potomac passed through Bristoe Station or camped for several days in fields around it. Captain George Lockley,

Company G of the 1st Michigan Volunteer Infantry, recorded in his diary on June 14, 1863: "Passed thro' the Village of Brenstville, (regular Virginia Village) and went about 2 miles to Kettle Run where we parked the wagons and bivouc'd for the night. . . . This has been a real warm and cloudy day. . . . A pretty long and hard march today. Some 30 miles. The men kept up finely. Took a swim in Kettle Run. Tired, stiff and sore. Roll'd myself in blanket." Just a week later, Sgt. James Kenney of the 1st Massachusetts Artillery recalled, "[A]nd on [June] 20th marched, passing over Centreville heights, by all the old Forts, on and over Bull Run field, past Manassas Junction and halted at Bristow Station." Kenney's artillery battery remained at Bristoe until June 25.

Still in Dumfries, Hooker wired Halleck with an outline of the Federal march to occur on June 15: "The First, Third, Sixth, and Eleventh Corps, with the cavalry, will be assembled at Manassas and Centreville to-night. The Second Corps will be at Dumfries, the Sixth at Wolf Run Shoals, and the Twelfth at Fairfax Court-House to-night." The I, III, and XI Corps constituted John Reynolds's wing of the army, and their marches of more than 25 miles— nearly 20 hours in column—were grueling. Not far behind was the V Corps, as well as the Federal cavalry, which pushed forward until it reached Manassas Junction. The movement of this wing continued to follow the Orange and Alexandria Railroad line.

Manassas Junction, Virginia, after its evacuation by the Confederates, March 1862. (loc)

Leave the parking lot and take a right at the traffic circle onto Iron Brigade Unit Avenue, then a left onto Route 619 (Bristow Road). Make your next right onto Route 28 north (Nokesville Road). Travel 1.1 miles and take Route 234 North (Prince William Parkway) towards Interstate 66. Travel on Route 234 north for 4.2 miles and take the right exit for Interstate 66 east. Travel 8.5 miles and take Exit 53 to Route 28 north (Sully Road). Stay on Route 29 north for 11.3

John Reynolds made his headquarters near Guilford Signal Station at the Lanesville house. The home, which dates back to the late 1700s, is named after the Lane family, which owned more than 1,000 acres. (dw)

Capt. Benjamin Fisher was the Army of the Potomac's chief acting signal officer during the Gettysburg campaign. Further complicating Gen. Hooker's ability to communicate, Fisher was captured near Aldie, Virginia, on June 17, 1863. (usamhi)

miles and take the right exit for Route 625 east (Church Road). In 0.7 miles, turn left onto Route 1794 (Cascades Parkway). In 1 mile take a right onto Old Vestals Gap Road (into Claude Moore Park–Historic Lanesville. The Civil War Trails marker will be between the two buildings on your left (near the parking lot). There is also a trail that takes you to the location of the signal station, where you can get a view of Sugarloaf Mountain in Maryland, the next signal station north of here.

GPS: N 39 °.019587 W 77 °.406104

STOP 7: GUILFORD STATION

On June 17, 1863, Gen. Reynolds sent a dispatch to Gen. Oliver O. Howard, informing the commander of the XI Corps, "I shall go to Guilford Station." Over the next forty-eight hours, Reynolds's corps of nearly 10,000 soldiers descended on Guilford. "I said above that we are now near Guilford Station, which you will not find on a common map unless you had a military map," George Cramer wrote to his wife several days later. "I will therfor state that its about, as far as I learned, nine miles south of Leisburg [sic]."

On his arrival, Reynolds established his headquarters at the Lanesville house. It was vital for Reynolds to reestablish constant contact with not only army headquarters, but as a wing commander, with his other commands and responsibilities. Meanwhile on the northern edge of the Lanesville property, Reynolds's men secured a 442-foot elevated position on which they erected a signal station. Essential for communications and for keeping an eye on Confederate activity, this was one of the highest points between Washington, D.C., and Leesburg, Virginia. Reynolds also had a telegraph line run from Guilford to Fairfax Court House, which further increased his ability to communicate with other commands and commanders.

Even with a complex signal station operation, Hooker had difficulties in his communication network. First, on June 17, Chief Acting Signal Officer Capt. Benjamin Fisher was captured near Aldie. Hooker did not effectively replace him during the campaign. Also, the command structure between Hooker and Federal forces in and around Washington made official communications cumbersome. Hooker did not have direct command over some of the men in the theater because they were not part of the Army of the Potomac. The forces in Harpers Ferry, for example, reported directly to Washington, so when Hooker received communications from the Federal forces there, it came through Washington first. Thus, Halleck and Lincoln were getting the most up-to-date information on Confederate whereabouts before Hooker received this intelligence. A frustrated Hooker nonetheless did little to alleviate these issues.

Receiving reports of Confederate forces north of the Potomac on June 24 via Harpers Ferry and other signal stations, Hooker ordered the Army of the Potomac to march towards Edwards Ferry in response. Hooker relayed his orders to Reynolds, who then made plans to move north. The Federals were still unsure of Lee's final objective. By the end of June 24, Reynolds's command left Guilford Station and moved toward Leesburg and the many river crossings near there.

Armies used signal stations as vital links in their communication chain during the Civil War. This signal station, a typical example, was on Elk Mountain in Maryland, overlooking the battlefield of Antietam in October 1862. (loc)

Exit the park and make a right onto Route 1794 (Cascades Parkway). Travel 0.9 miles and take the second right exit ramp onto Route 7 west (Harry Byrd Highway). Travel 6.2 miles and take a right onto Route 659 north (Belmont Ridge Road). In 0.5 miles, make a left onto Riverpoint Drive. Remain on Riverpoint Drive for 1 mile (you will be driving through a large residential area, so please be cautious). Make a left into the parking area for Kephart Bridge Park. There will be a Civil War Trails marker in the parking lot. To view the site of Edwards Ferry and the Union crossing locations on the Potomac River, follow the trail from the parking lot and follow along the Goose Creek Canal trail towards the Potomac. It will be a 2-mile round trip walk.

GPS: N 39°.098517 W 77°.494430

STOP 8: EDWARDS FERRY
BY CRAIG SWAIN

When the XII Corps arrived in Leesburg, the army faced a tenuous logistical position. Unable to secure the road from Leesburg to Vienna, XII Corps commander Maj. Gen. Henry Slocum suggested the army use the Chesapeake and Ohio (C&O) Canal. "Edwards Ferry is most accessible, and is covered by

Capt. Samuel Fiske of the 14th Connecticut Volunteer Infantry recorded his regiment's experience crossing the pontoon bridges at Edwards Ferry in late June 1863. (loc)

a strong redoubt on this side. Our supplies should be sent from Georgetown, by canal, to Edwards Ferry," wrote the general. Hooker approved construction of a pontoon bridge at Edwards Ferry to facilitate the supply line, and by the morning of June 21, the 1,340-foot pontoon bridge upstream of the mouth of Goose Creek was completed.

Captain Charles Turnbull's engineers then built a short bridge over Goose Creek at the landing. The intention was to use that bridge over the creek to supply those elements behind Goose Creek. Though a minor detail, the bridge was an important arrangement. At that time, Goose Creek cut across the Army of the Potomac's sector. With no other bridges along the course of the creek, save one fabricated at the Alexandria-Leesburg Turnpike crossing, that short pontoon section at Edwards Ferry offered a vital link between the halves of the army.

When the need arose to move elements of the army across the Potomac, Hooker's staff issued directions to increase the capacity of bridging at Edwards Ferry. Hooker soon called for the laying of a second pontoon bridge. However, those orders lacked important details: specifically, whether the second bridge would be upstream or downstream of the first. Furthermore, the engineers at Edwards Ferry, at mid-day on June 24, did not have all the necessary materials to lay a second bridge. Lastly, the original pontoon bridge, in heavy use by supply trains, was in need of maintenance. These issues, along with the countermanding of orders, imposed significant delays during the day to follow. Adding to the woes, Hooker countermanded movement orders for the XI Corps, further imposing delays to the river crossing.

Taking some initiative, Turnbull determined to put in the second pontoon bridge in absence of a response from headquarters. "[H]aving received no instructions," he wrote at 11 am, "I have put the second bridge on the south side of Goose Creek." The engineers worked through mid-day, and the second pontoon bridge was completed shortly after 2 p.m. on June 25. The I Corps began crossing soon thereafter. The III Corps followed the XI Corps's path to the upper bridge. Compounding the complications and delays, rain fell that afternoon. The muddy approaches to the bridges hindered the I and III corps's crossings.

On June 26, Hooker's orders called for the XII Corps to march down from Leesburg and cross on the upper bridge, followed by the V Corps coming up from Aldie. The Artillery Reserve crossed on the morning of June 26. Hooker's headquarters element followed the artillery. That afternoon, the II Corps reached Edwards Ferry and prepared to cross. As Captain Samuel Fiske of the 14th Connecticut recalled, his regiment started a movement to the bridge at 9 p.m. It should have taken an hour to cross, but not until after midnight did they get to the far side. On the Maryland bank, they waited on the roads for two or three more hours before receiving orders to camp out in a field. As Fiske later recalled, "So here was the hour's work accomplished in the course of the night by making three removes of camp, and at the trifling expense of a night's rest to the troops between two days' marches, and with the ultimate result of getting the same exhausted troops to Frederick City a day later than they were ordered and expected."

Even with two bridges in place, congestion and delays continued to slow the army's crossing, but by June 27, the trailing formations of the army crossed Edwards Ferry. Despite these issues, the army had crossed over 90,000 men, tens of thousands of wagons, cavalry, and livestock in just two and a half days while at the same time having built one bridge in record time. The last infantry column reached Edwards Ferry around 3 p.m. and crossed over the Potomac that evening. At 8:35 p.m., Brig. Gen. Henry Benham, commanding the Engineer Brigade, reported that all the infantry was across and that Gregg's cavalry was following. By midnight on June 27, the Army of the Potomac completed its crossing of the Potomac. With the last cavalryman to cross, Benham's mind turned to withdrawal of the bridges. By the morning of June 28, all the bridges were recovered.

River crossing operations are among the most complex performed by a field army. That was especially true at Edwards Ferry in June 1863. The engineers laid the first bridge to provide a secure supply line. Later, when the army crossed the Potomac, confusing orders, traffic control problems,

Today, the Edwards Ferry pontoon crossing site is only accessible on the Virginia side via a trail in Kephart Bridge Landing. (cs)

weather, and friction slowed the crossing. These delays cost valuable time for the army marching in pursuit of the Confederates. But at the same time, the movement over the Potomac at Edwards Ferry enabled success at Gettysburg. The first three infantry corps to cross the river, constituting Reynolds's wing, were the first to arrive in Adams County, Pennsylvania. Most of the Federal troops who fought at Gettysburg crossed those pontoon bridges.

Turn right out of the park entrance and travel 0.6 miles to make a right onto Kipheart Drive. Travel 0.3 miles and make a right onto Riverside Parkway. Stay on Riverside Parkway for 2.8 miles (Riverside Parkway will become Fort Evans Road) and make a right onto Route 15 north.

There are two ways to access Poolesville, Maryland. You can take a ferry across the Potomac River. To do so, travel 3.1 miles and make a right onto Route 655 (Whites Ferry Road). There is a small fee to ride the ferry, which is the last working ferry across the Potomac River. Once across the river, Poolesville is about 6 miles to the east. To take the traditional route, stay on Route 15 north for 13.8 miles into Maryland and make your first right once you cross the Potomac River onto Route 28 (Clay Street). Remain on Route 28 for 4.7 miles and make a right to remain on Route 28 (Dickerson Road). Continue on Route 28 for 7 miles entering the village of Beallsville and make a right onto Route 109 south (Beallsville Road). Travel 2.4 miles, enter the town of Poolesville, and make a left onto Fisher Avenue. On your immediate left will be a side street with two Civil War Trails markers. The one near the end of the street focuses on the Gettysburg campaign.

GPS: N 39 °.146196 W 77 °.415497

STOP 9: POOLESVILLE

Before the Federal army crossed at Edwards Ferry, large portions of the Federal column rested. By June 23 and into June 24, 1863, however, the Army of the Potomac stirred once again. During the next two days, headquarters for the army were established at one of the first towns across the Potomac River in Maryland. Between June 25 and June 27, four of the seven infantry corps in the Army of the Potomac, as well as the cavalry corps and the army's artillery reserve marched through the town. Hooker arrived at the temporary army headquarters at Poolesville in the evening of June 26.

This was not the first time war had come to Poolesville. Union soldiers occupied the town for the previous year before the Gettysburg campaign. Also, Poolesville served as another link in the signal station and flag signal lines between the I Corps at Guilford Station, the XI Corps at Trappe Rock, the XII Corps at Leesburg, as well as other signal stations at Sugar Loaf Mountain, Point of Rocks, and Maryland Heights.

Surely Hooker, while he was in town, and the thousands of Federal soldiers marching through would have seen the oldest building, constructed by John Poole, Jr., in 1793. The structure served as a trading post and originally consisted of one room, with a loft upstairs. Just two decades later, the first of several additions was constructed. With Hooker's arrival, the need for broadening the communication links with other portions of the army increased. When Hooker left Poolesville at 9:00 a.m. on June 27, the army's headquarters were in the saddle.

Commanding the XII Corps during the Gettysburg campaign, Maj. Gen. Henry Slocum was a West Point graduate and prewar lawyer. Slocum had risen through the ranks of the Army of the Potomac, reaching the rank of major general by the summer of 1862. Despite early praise during the war, Slocum was heavily criticized for the amount of time it took for his command to reach Gettysburg. (loc)

Turn around and get back on Route 109 north (Elgin Road/ Beallsville Road). Travel 6 miles and make a left onto Barnesville Road. In 0.2 miles, the Civil War Trails marker will be on your left in the parking lot for the St. Mary's Catholic Shrine.

GPS: N 39 °.221196 W 77 °.381441

STOP 10: BARNESVILLE

In September 1862, Confederate cavalry bivouacked near the town, and just days later a running skirmish between Union and Confederate cavalry erupted through the heart of the town. Now, once again, soldiers and war returned to Barnesville. On the morning of June 26, the I Corps, after crossing the Potomac River at Edwards Ferry the previous afternoon, trudged through Barnesville at a terribly slow pace. Heavy

A modern image of St. Mary's Catholic Church depicts the church as it has looked for many decades in the twentieth century. Although the current structure was not the one Federal soldiers saw in June 1863, it sits on the same ground. Following the war, several Civil War veterans were later interred in the church cemetery. (dw)

Maj. Gen. Winfield Scott Hancock commanded the Army of the Potomac's II Corps during the Gettysburg campaign. Hancock, a West Point graduate and career army officer, had risen steadily in rank in the volunteer army since 1861. The Gettysburg campaign was Hancock's first time as a corps commander. (loc)

rains turned the roads and nearby fields to bogs, hampering forward progress. The following day, although the weather cleared, it was still a tough march through Barnesville and the area to the north. Townspeople this day saw soldiers of the II Corps under Maj. Gen. Winfield Scott Hancock pass through the town; twenty-four hours later, Maj. Gen. John Sedgwick's VI Corps marched through. June 28 was a Sunday, and the men of the VI Corps had the opportunity to hear prayers for President Lincoln and peace at St. Mary's Catholic Church. Although the church that stands here today was built in 1900, the cemetery in the rear of this church holds the postwar graves of several Civil War veterans.

Take a left out of the parking lot and continue on Barnesville Road for 1.9 miles and turn left onto Mt. Ephraim Road. Travel 0.5 miles and make a right onto Mouth of Monocacy Road. Continue on Mouth of Monocacy Road for 1.7 miles until you reach the parking lot for the Monocacy Aqueduct. The Civil War Trails marker here is for the Antietam campaign; you can gain access to the Monocacy Aqueduct from the parking lot.

GPS: N 39 °.222557 W 77 °.450169

STOP 11: MONOCACY AQUEDUCT

The entire Federal army was on the march on June 26. Reynolds's wing moved towards the western mountain gaps and approaches to Frederick, Maryland. The security of these gaps, including Crampton's and Boonesborough, was assigned to several XI Corps units.

An 1861 *Harper's Weekly* woodcut engraving of the Monocacy Aqueduct. (loc)

The XI Corps's progress on June 26 marked the farthest point north for the Federal army and Reynolds' wing. The I Corps came to rest near Jefferson, Maryland, while the III Corps—Maj. Gen. Daniel Sickles, commanding—marched along the Baltimore and Ohio (B&O) Railroad towards Point of Rocks. The middle of the Federal column, the XII Corps, crossed Edwards Ferry during the day and pushed on until they reached the Monocacy Aqueduct.

Benjamin Wright served as chief engineer on the C&O Canal and the Monocacy Aqueduct. (fw)

Completed in 1833, the 516-foot span took four years and 200 workers to complete. Chief Engineer Benjamin Wright, who also worked as an engineer on the Erie Canal, was placed in charge of the construction of the C&O Canal. His plans for the Monocacy Aqueduct called for it to be not only functional, but also grand and ornamental, with different-colored stones. Two years after its completion, an annual report by the C&O Canal Company noted, "Aqueduct No. 2, over the Monocacy River, is a very splendid work, built of a superior granite stone, resembling white marble." Confederate soldiers tried to blow up this "very splendid work" several times during the 1862 Maryland campaign.

XII Corps soldiers saw this splendid work on June 26 during the Gettysburg campaign. Joseph Irwin, a soldier in a XII Corps regiment, remembered crossing here: "Crossed the Monocacy, by the aquedoc [*sic*]," he recalled. We "[m]arched up the towpath several miles, then crossed under the canal by a means of a culvert." By the close of June 26, a majority of both armies were across the Potomac River, despite Lee's ignorance of this development in the Federal advance. It was a major obstacle for both columns during their forward movement, thus, the tempo of the campaign now increased and, with it, the looming and growing possibility of large and sustained combat.

Leave the parking lot and continue on Mouth of Monocacy Road for 1.3 miles and make a left onto Route 28 (Dickerson Road). Continue on Route 28 for 3.3 miles and make a left to stay on Route 28 (Tuscarora Road). Travel 4.2 miles on Route 28 (continuing into the town of Point of Rocks) and make a left into the parking lot of the Point of Rocks MARC station. Two Civil War Trails markers are located in the median facing the train station.

GPS: N 39 °.273846 W 77 °.533683

Lt. Col. John S. Mosby was just one Confederate officer that led a raid on Point of Rocks, Maryland, during the American Civil War. He would also help plan Stuart's controversial ride during the Gettysburg campaign. (loc)

STOP 12: POINT OF ROCKS

While Reynolds's wing moved towards the western mountain gaps and approaches to Frederick, Maryland, and with the XII Corps at the Monocacy Aqueduct, the III Corps marched along the B&O Railroad toward Point of Rocks. During the 1830s, as construction of the B&O Railroad and the C&O Canal pushed westward, these two modes of transportation eventually reached the narrow passageway between the Catoctin Mountains and the Potomac River; thus, both the B&O and C&O lines came to an end at Point of Rocks. With the end of these lines came the development of a small town nearby, which took its name from the geologic feature.

The importance of both of these lines continued up to and during the American Civil War. Point of Rocks was the subject of two Confederate raids during the war: the first raid by Stonewall Jackson in May 1861 and the second by Lt. Col. John Mosby in 1864. Also at Point of Rocks stood an important link in the Federal communication structure, a signal station located north of town on Catoctin Ridge. The station could relay messages from Maryland Heights (Harpers Ferry) to Sugarloaf Mountain or directly to Guilford Station in Virginia.

At the end of the second week of the Gettysburg campaign, no further B & O trains moved west of Point of Rocks because of rumors that the Confederate army was invading Maryland. Their caution was warranted. On June 17, Confederate cavalry crossed the Potomac River and not only attacked Union cavalry nearby but also captured a Union military train at Point of Rocks. The train's cargo was burned while the train's engineer, conductor, and more than a dozen passengers were captured. The raid sent shock waves of fear and anxiety throughout Maryland, including in nearby Frederick. Just ten days later, however, the uniforms of those passing through Point of Rocks changed. Thousands of Union soldiers, such as those in the Federal III Corps, passed through the town on their way northward. Point of Rocks was yet another point along the route northward for a portion of the Army of the Potomac.

Turn left out of the parking lot and drive 0.5 miles to take a right onto Route 15 north. Continue on Route 15 for 4.8 miles and make a left onto Mountville Road. Stay on Mountville Road for 2 miles and make a right onto Lander Road. In 0.1 miles make a right onto a frontage road facing Route 340. The Civil War Trails marker is on your right in the median (across from the gas station).

GPS: N 39 °.360375 W 77 °.531659

STOP 13: JEFFERSON

By the end of June 26, 1863, Reynolds's I Corps came to rest near Jefferson, Maryland. The command also included the III and XI Corps. This wing of the Army of the Potomac operated in the area during this part of the Gettysburg campaign because Hooker still did not know his adversary's full intentions and felt strongly that Lee and the Army of Northern Virginia would try to push through the gaps in the South Mountain range. The Federal units needed to protect and hold such places as Crampton's, Turner's, and Fox's gaps. These gaps had also played a key role in the Maryland campaign in the fall of 1862.

J. Henry Blakeman had been with the 17th Connecticut Volunteer Infantry less than a year before the start of the Gettysburg campaign. He would be wounded during the fighting at Gettysburg and later transferred to Baltimore, Maryland, to recover. (gnmp)

To reach the gaps, Union soldiers had to march through Maryland towns such as Jefferson and Burkittsville. Residents of these pro-Union towns received their guests with great pomp and circumstance, hanging and waving flags, feeding the men and refilling canteens. J. Henry Blakeman of the 17th Connecticut Volunteer Infantry, an XI Corps regiment, wrote to his mother about it on June 27, 1863: "The people about seem to be good union almost unanimously," he said. "[A]s we passed through Jefferson and Middletown we saw flags to almost every house women waving handkerchiefs and seeming very much pleased to see our troops pas through.—it seemed as different from the cold reception we always met in Virginia and the actions of the soldiers are proportionately different."

Meanwhile, the right wing of the army endured marches just as long and arduous as the left wing. The II Corps marched from Gum Spring, Virginia, over the Potomac River to Frederick, before ending its day, while the VI Corps collected its divisions from Bristoe and Germantown and moved up Hunter Mill Road towards Dranesville, Virginia, site of a December 1861 fight between Union and Confederate forces.

Today, a Civil War Trails marker sits just outside modern Jefferson, Maryland, detailing the town's involvement in the Gettysburg campaign. (dw)

Here they camped for the evening and marched for the crossing site of the Potomac the following morning. Federal cavalry occupied Leesburg and Frederick on June 26. Hooker's objective for the Federal army this day was a concentration near Middletown and Frederick, Maryland, only miles apart from each other.

Turn right on Lander Road and then take your next right onto Route 180 east (Jefferson Pike). Continue on Route 180 east for 5.9 miles and make a left onto Himes Avenue. Turn immediately left onto Mansion Drive. Two Civil War Trails markers are on your right at the intersection with Mansion Drive with a monument to Meade (a boulder from Devil's Den). Prospect Hall is to your left.

GPS: N 39 °.403776 W 77 °.438885

STOP 14: PROSPECT HALL

Communications to and from Washington began early for General Hooker on June 27. At 8:00 a.m. Lincoln wired the general a follow-up to a conversation that had lasted for days. At about that time, Hooker composed yet another missive to General Halleck about the disparity of numbers of men in the ranks that Hooker perceived: "That there may be no misunderstanding as to my force, I would respectfully state that . . . my whole force of enlisted men for duty will not exceed 105,000," wrote Hooker. He wanted to make it clear that he felt that he did not have enough men. To accomplish the objectives for the campaign, as laid out by Halleck and Lincoln, Hooker wanted to fold more troops into the army from Washington and the Federal garrison at Harpers Ferry. "I state these facts that there may not be expected of me more than I have material to do with," Hooker wrote. By 10:30 a.m., Halleck responded. He wanted it to be clear to Hooker that he was not going to be getting any more reinforcements—from either Washington or Harpers

Ferry. Both of these locations were vital to the strategic Federal operations, and Halleck felt they had already been stripped down enough. "Maryland Heights [at Harpers Ferry] have always been regarded as an important point to be held by us," Halleck wrote, "and much expense and labor incurred in fortifying them. I cannot approve their abandonment. . . ."

Hooker had reached the zenith of his frustration with Halleck and Lincoln: too few troops and too many, far-flung strategic objectives imposed on him. "My original instructions require me to cover Harper's Ferry and Washington. I have now imposed upon me, in addition, an enemy in my front of more than my number . . . . I am unable to comply with this condition with the means at my disposal, and earnestly request that I may at once be relieved from the position I occupy."

At 8:00 p.m., Halleck wired Hooker that he had received the request, and "As you were appointed to this command by the President, I have no power to relieve you. Your dispatch has been duly referred for Executive action." June 27 came to an end with a serious decision for Lincoln.

A decision reached Hooker's camp only hours later. During the predawn hours of June 28, Col. James Hardie, Assistant Adjutant General on Halleck's staff entered the headquarters of the V Corps with orders for Maj. Gen. George Gordon Meade. Those orders, which were penned late on the evening of the 27th, placed Meade in command of the Army of the Potomac. "Considering the circumstances, no one ever received a more important command," Halleck wrote; "and I cannot doubt that you will fully justify the confidence which the Government has reposed in you." After dressing, Meade and Hardie went to Hooker's headquarters where Fightin' Joe was relieved as commander of the Army of the Potomac on the grounds of Prospect Hall.

Lincoln and Halleck made an excellent choice. Meade was a West Point graduate and career army officer, his star rose leading men in the Civil War. Eventually Meade commanded the V Corps. Even with all of Meade's qualifications, Lincoln believed that as the situation reflected a serious Confederate threat to the state of Pennsylvania, Meade, a native Pennsylvanian, would "fight well on his own dung hill."

Meade wired back to Halleck at 7:00 a.m.: "The

Maj. Gen. George G. Meade, born in Cádiz, Spain, and raised in Pennsylvania, was a West Point graduate and veteran of the Seminole and Mexican Wars. Meade left the army for a brief period to pursue a civilian career as a civil engineer. He performed well on the battlefields of the Civil War and steadily rose through the ranks, receiving promotion to command the Army of Potomac by President Lincoln on June 28, 1863. (loc)

Col. James A. Hardie, assistant adjutant general on Halleck's staff, was tasked with delivering the orders for Gen. Meade to take command of the Army of the Potomac. (loc)

Construction of Prospect Hall began in 1787 and was not completed until 1810. Built by Daniel Dulaney, a landowner with significant tracts in Frederick County, Maryland, Prospect Hall has had many uses since June 28, 1863. (dw)

order placing me in command of this army is received. As a soldier, I obey it, and to the utmost of my ability will execute it."

The order that promoted Meade to command of the army also imposed several conditions on the general. First, the army must always act as the covering army for Washington and Baltimore, as well "as the army of operation against the invading forces of the rebels." In addition, Meade was expected to give Lee battle. Outside of these stipulations, Meade had full control of garrisons and other commands in which his army operated (including Harpers Ferry), the authority to remove and appoint officers within the army, and generally command without "any minute instructions from these headquarters." When Meade wired back to Halleck the receipt of the orders, he honestly told the general-in-chief of his ignorance to the condition of the army and the position of the enemy. One thing Meade did know, which he relayed to Washington: the army must get back on the march.

Turn around and take Himes Avenue back to Route 180 and make a left onto Route 180, then take the exit for Route 15 north (Jefferson Street)—BUT DO NOT continue on Route 15 north towards Gettysburg; rather, stay straight on Jefferson

Street into downtown Frederick. Stay on South Jefferson Street
for 1.1 miles and make a right onto South Street. Travel for
0.7 miles on South Street and take a left onto South Carroll
Street. In 0.2 miles, take a left onto East Patrick Street. The
National Museum of Civil War Medicine will be on your left.
There is street parking as well as the Carroll Creek Parking
Deck next to the museum. While in downtown Frederick,
there are two Civil War Trails markers that pertain to the
Gettysburg campaign. The National Museum of Civil War
Medicine is an excellent place to visit, as well.

Parking/Downtown Frederick:
GPS: N 39 °.414022 W 77 °.409364

Patrick and Market Street Civil War Trails Marker:
GPS: N 39 °.414170 W 77 °.410760

North Market Street Civil War Trails Marker:
GPS: N 39 °.415969 W 77 °.410678

STOP 15: DOWNTOWN FREDERICK

Hooker had made Frederick a concentration point bringing the scattered wings of the Army of the Potomac together again after days of operating separately. As the events of June 27-28 unfolded, however, Hooker was no longer in command, and the army marked time at Frederick while Meade, the new commanding general, engineered a plan for the army. Meade's first instructions were to Reynolds, who was to abandon the defense of the mountain passes and march his wing to Frederick. Meade ordered the continued concentration of the army near the town. That night, the II and XII Corps ended their march of June 28 within site of the town, even as the VI Corps plodded northward through Poolesville, Barnesville, and Hyattstown, Maryland.

The cavalry was also on the move. General Buford's division scoured the valley between Middletown and Boonsboro for signs of the Confederate army while Pleasonton ordered Gregg's command to search for the elusive Stuart and protect the B&O Railroad and the telegraph lines that ran alongside it.

While in Frederick and its nearby environs, many soldiers took the opportunity to visit stores and homes to buy fresh bread, milk, and other sundries the army did not supply or which sutlers overcharged for. These

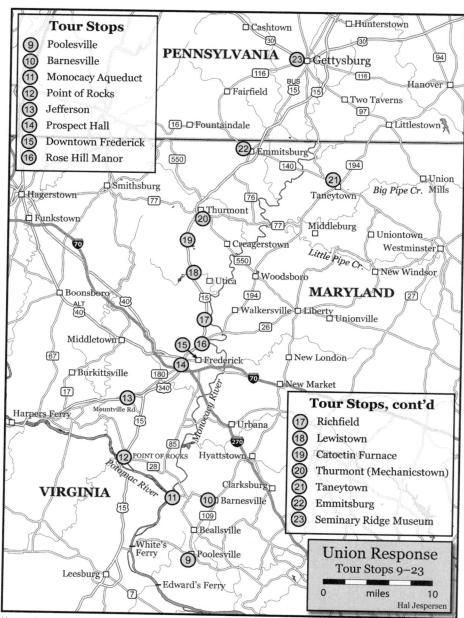

Tour Stops

- ⑨ Poolesville
- ⑩ Barnesville
- ⑪ Monocacy Aqueduct
- ⑫ Point of Rocks
- ⑬ Jefferson
- ⑭ Prospect Hall
- ⑮ Downtown Frederick
- ⑯ Rose Hill Manor

Tour Stops, cont'd

- ⑰ Richfield
- ⑱ Lewistown
- ⑲ Catoctin Furnace
- ⑳ Thurmont (Mechanicstown)
- ㉑ Taneytown
- ㉒ Emmitsburg
- ㉓ Seminary Ridge Museum

Union Response
Tour Stops 9–23

0   miles   10

Hal Jespersen

UNION RESPONSE—The second half of the Union Response tour will follow several corps of the Army of the Potomac after their crossing of the Potomac River northward. The route will end on the first day's battlefield at Gettysburg.

were not the only places men in the ranks visited, though. The town's bars and taverns did a roaring business while the army was in the area. Many accounts recall the drunkenness of soldiers in the Army of the Potomac while in Frederick. Not all partook in the frivolities that liquor provided, though. Some soldiers with relatives in and around Frederick took an opportunity to visit their loved ones. One such soldier was none other than Reynolds himself. The general visited briefly with his cousin Catherine and her sisters before he headed to a meeting with Gen. Meade. It was the last time John's cousins ever saw him.

From Patrick Street, take North Market Street (Route 355), travel 1.5 miles, and make a left into the entrance for Rose Hill Manor Park and Children's Museum. The Civil War Trails marker will be on the right along the entrance road.

GPS: N 39 °.435802 W 77 °.405579

STOP 16: ROSE HILL MANOR

As the Union army concentrated near Frederick, one can imagine everything they brought with them. In addition to the approximately 95,000 men in the ranks, the army traveled with lengthy columns of wagons filled with food, ammunition, and other accouterments of war. Also in those columns were livestock to be butchered and dispersed amongst the troops. Medical supplies and ambulance wagons were also in the line. Thousands upon thousands of horses—used to pull the wagons, artillery, and by officers and, of course, the cavalry—filled the ranks, as well. Further adding to the column's length were the hundreds of cannons, caissons, forges, and other needed items for the army's artillery.

Not only did the Army of the Potomac have artillery assigned to each of its seven corps, it also had a reserve from which to draw during times of intense

Rose Hill Manor now serves as a local history and children's museum. (dw)

The nephew of Union Gen. Daniel Tyler—who also played a role in the Gettysburg campaign—Brig. Gen. Robert Tyler (above)—served as the commanding officer of the Army of the Potomac's large Artillery Reserve. (loc)

combat. Hooker created this reserve following the battle of Chancellorsville as one of the many organizational changes made during May 1863. Commanded by Brig. Gen. Robert Tyler (during the army's time around Frederick), the nineteen reserve Federal batteries consisted of 110 cannons, more than 2,000 horses, 3,000 men, and hundreds of caissons, traveling forges, and ammunition wagons. They all parked at Rose Hill Manor, which had ample ground. When the Artillery Reserve finally moved northward with the army, the damage to the property—and the clean-up effort that ensured—was immense.

Take a left out of the park onto Route 355 north (North Market Street) and, in 1 mile, stay right to merge onto Route 26 (Liberty Road). Make your immediate left (in 0.3 miles) onto Monocacy Boulevard. Continue on Monocacy Boulevard for 1.2 miles and make a right onto Route 15 north. Travel 0.6 miles and take a right onto Willow Road. The Civil War Trails marker will be on your right facing Route 15.

GPS: N 39 °.468545 W 77 °.401330

STOP 17: RICHFIELD

When Meade took command of the Army of the Potomac on June 28, his first instructions were all directed towards the seven army corps under his command. He wanted to get the army up and marching again and close the yawning gap between it and the Army of Northern Virginia. With the army on the march, Meade also worked to reorganize the cavalry. Hooker had transferred Maj. Gen. Julius Stahel to the Department of the Susquehanna just hours before he was relieved from command of the army, but since the change in army commanders, Meade was left to finish the job. Pleasonton discussed with Meade several options to reorganize the arm and Meade took those suggestions. To replace Stahel, Brig. Gen. Judson Kilpatrick took command of the Third Division of the Federal cavalry. Meade, as authorized in his orders, also promoted several young captains to the rank of brigadier general. Captains Elon Farnsworth, Wesley Merritt and George Custer all received promotions and their own brigades.

Brig. Gen. Elon Farnsworth, Meade's second cavalry promotion, only held this post for days before getting killed in action on July 3, 1863. Farnsworth's promotion from captain to brigadier general was preceded by Merritt's similar rise in rank. (phocw)

Brig. Gen. Judson Kilpatrick graduated from West Point after the war had already begun. He saw service in the artillery and infantry arms before serving in the arm that would bring him fame, the cavalry. (loc)

The most famous of Meade's promotions during the Gettysburg campaign, Brig. Gen. George Custer, would prove to be a hard fighter over the next few days at Gettysburg. (loc)

Newly minted brigadier Wesley Merritt began the Gettysburg campaign as a captain in command of the First Reserve Brigade in the army's cavalry corps. On June 29, General Meade promoted Merritt from captain to brigadier general, a rare jump in rank in the Army of the Potomac. (loc)

After their promotion on June 29, newly minted Generals Custer and Farnsworth rode north out of Frederick. They assumed their new commands the next day at Richfield where their men were camped. During the rest of June 29, the I and XI Corps marched past Richfield, and more than a week later, during the pursuit of the retreating Confederate army, Meade passed by the property, as well. Unfortunately, the home that stands at Richfield today is not the home that stood during the Gettysburg campaign. It was destroyed by a tornado in 1929.

A Civil War Trails marker at Richfield also highlights a visit to the area by George Washington. (cm)

Return to Route 15 north. Travel 5.1 miles and make a right onto Fish Hatchery Road. In 0.5 miles, make a right onto Hessong Bridge Road. The Civil War Trails marker will be on your right in front of the Lewistown United Methodist Church.

GPS: N 39 °.537415 W 77 °.415653

STOP 18: LEWISTOWN

"We marched from Frederick City to Emmitsburg, passing on the way through Lewistown . . ." Capt. Emanuel Roath of the 107th Pennsylvania Volunteer Infantry wrote. "Having marched all day in rain and mud . . . the men were much fatigued on the march." Although much of the campaign through the end of June had been hot and dry, June 29 proved to be a wet and challenging day for the men on the march. The first units through Lewistown that day were from Reynolds's I Corps. Further units from Reynolds' wing of the army continued to march through Lewistown throughout the day. They left their bivouac earlier that morning west of Frederick and were ordered to reach Emmitsburg nearly twenty-three miles away by the end of the day.

This was not the last time that residents of Lewistown saw men of the Army of the Potomac. Brigades of Federal cavalry rendezvoused at Lewistown following the battle of Gettysburg. "On the 4th and 5th," wrote Brig. Gen. Wesley Merritt, "we marched to Lewistown, from near Gettysburg, to Frederick City, where the brigade joined the division, from which it had been temporarily detached." On July 7, during the pursuit of Lee's retreating army, three of the seven army corps—the I, VI, and XI—also marched through the area until they turned westward, heading towards the Catoctin Mountain range and into the Middletown Valley beyond.

Return to Route 15 north by turning left on Hessong Bridge Road. Then take a left on Fish Hatchery Road. Take a right onto Route 15 north and travel for 2.5 miles and make a right onto Route 806 (Catoctin Furnace Road). In 0.7 miles, make a left into the parking lot for Catoctin Furnace. The Civil War Trails marker is located in the parking lot.

GPS: N 39°.581108 W 77°.434110

STOP 19: CATOCTIN FURNACE

With the vanguard of the Army of the Potomac's left wing on the march on June 29, numerous Maryland towns witnessed Union soldiers trudging northward. The Army of the Potomac's I Corps was leading the way that day through Frederick, past Richfield, and through Lewistown. Although many of these towns turned out for the honor of seeing the Union army pass through, workers at Catoctin Furnace were too busy to do so. The charcoal furnaces, owned by John Baker Kunkel, were operating full blast on June 29. During the war, the Catoctin Furnace produced three tons of pig iron a day through round-the-clock twelve-hour shifts for its workers. The vital pig iron was then shipped eastward to arsenals and forges used in the production of weapons and materials for the Union war effort. Units of the Army of the Potomac marched by the furnace again during Lee's retreat. Brigadier General Joseph Bartlett, commanding a brigade in the VI Corps, wrote on July 7, "Marched at an early hour in the morning, and, after passing Catoctin Furnace, took a road to the right, leading over the Catoctin Mountain."

This furnace stack and casting shed, "Isabella," was the second of three stacks built at Catoctin Furnace and was completed in 1858. It was running hot as Union soldiers marched by on their way north into Pennsylvania. (dw)

Take a left out of the parking area, continue on Catoctin Furnace Road for 0.5 miles, and make a left to access Route 15 north. Travel on Route 15 north for 2.7 miles and take the exit for Route 77. At the bottom of the exit ramp, make a left onto Route 77 east (Main Street). Travel 0.2 miles to downtown Thurmont. The Civil War Trails marker is on your left in the small park at the corner of Main Street and North Church Street.

GPS: N 39 °.623890 W 77 °.411629

STOP 20: THURMONT (MECHANICSTOWN)

The I Corps's march would not end until it reached Emmitsburg on June 29. The next town the I Corps passed through after Catoctin Furnace was Mechanicstown—modern-day Thurmont. In addition to the Union infantry that marched through the town, Merritt's cavalry brigade was ordered to stay here as a rearguard for the Federal army. The rest of the left wing of the Army of Potomac would also march through its environs in the coming days.

In many towns in northern Maryland and south-central Pennsylvania during late June 1863, rumors swirled regarding the location and intent of the Confederate army and what their own army was doing to stop them. So, too, Mechanicstown's citizens were fraught with such rumors, leaving some residents to leave town with what they could. Those who did leave later felt justified when, after the battle of Gettysburg and during the retreat of the Army of Northern Virginia, Jeb Stuart and his division of cavalry arrived on the outskirts of town. Stuart's men and mounts were still exhausted from their ride around the Army of the Potomac and the July 3 battle east of Gettysburg. Now, on July 5, Stuart rested his men and fed and watered his horses at a grain mill just outside of the town. They did not stay long. After receiving intelligence of Union cavalry operating in the area, Stuart put his column back on the road. Union forces arrived back in town later that day. Lieutenant Colonel Porter Tripp of the 11th Massachusetts Volunteer Infantry recorded in his official report of the Gettysburg campaign, "We remained near Gettysburg until the morning of the 5th instant, when we marched back through Emmitsburg, and encamped for the night at Mechanicstown, a distance of 18 miles from Gettysburg. [We] left Mechanicstown [the] next morning. . . ."

Modern day Thurmont, Maryland, was originally known as Mechanicstown. A small memorial park recognizes the town's history and includes several plaques and markers, just outside the frame, in the town's center. (dw)

From the Civil War Trails marker, take East Main Street for 1 mile and turn left onto Route 77 east (Rocky Ridge Road) for 9.2 miles to Keymar Maryland. Take a left onto Route 194 (Francis Scott Key Highway) and travel 5.3 miles (into Taneytown) and make a left onto Route 140 (West Baltimore Street). In 0.3 miles, the entrance to Taneytown Memorial Park will be on your left. The Civil War Trails marker (and two other historic markers) is located at the park entrance.

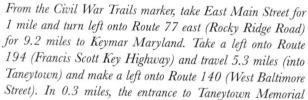

GPS: N 39 °.663258 W 77 °.180676— Taneytown

Though not an official stop on the tour, the nearby Loys Station Covered Bridge is an interesting site. To reach the covered bridge from the Thurmont stop, travel 2.4 miles on Route 77 (Rocky Ridge Road) and make a right onto Old Frederick Road. In 0.4 miles the road will cross the covered bridge. The parking lot and Civil War Trails marker for the bridge is on your right once you cross the bridge.

GPS: N 39 °.608203 W 77 °.351956—Loys Station Covered Bridge

Another slight detour on the way to Taneytown will lead you to the Pipe Creek Line. Here was Meade's potential defensive position to block a possible advance by Lee towards Washington or Baltimore. The Pipe Creek line also served as a possible fallback position for the Army of the Potomac if events at Gettysburg dictated a reverse. To reach the Pipe Creek Civil War Trails marker, travel 9.2 miles on Route 77 (Rocky Ridge Road). Continue straight on Middleburg Road, travel 0.9 miles and the Civil War Trails marker is on your left.

GPS: N 39 °.595508 W 77 °.223581—Pipe Creek

STOP 21: TANEYTOWN

Taneytown was yet another northern Maryland town that lay in the path of elements of the Army of the Potomac during the final days of June 1863. Taneytown continued to see Union soldiers, including the I and II Corps, march hard to reach a growing battle in nearby Adams County, Pennsylvania, that erupted on July 1. The small town also served as Meade's headquarters during the final phases of the Union advance. Meade established his headquarters here on June 29 and continued to oversee army operations from Taneytown during June 30 and July 1. Meade learned of the death of Gen. Reynolds during the morning fight on July 1 here, and from here he issued orders to Winfield Scott Hancock to proceed to Gettysburg and take command of all Union soldiers on the field in Meade's absence. Near 10:00 p.m., after a full day of battle and the defeat of the Federal I and XI Corps, Meade and his staff were in the saddle, headed north on the Taneytown Road, toward Gettysburg and battle.

Take a left out of the park entrance onto Route 140 (West Baltimore Street). Continue on Route 140 for 8.4 miles (entering into Emmitsburg) then take a left onto South Seton Avenue. In 0.4 miles turn left into the National Shrine of St. Elizabeth Ann Seton. The Civil War Trails markers are in the median of the parking lot to your left.

GPS: N 39 °.698904 W 77 °.327410

STOP 22: EMMITSBURG

Twenty-four hours into his command, Meade showed no signs of hesitation and continued to push his army hard to bridge the large geographical gap that had developed between the Army of the Potomac and the Army of Northern Virginia. The Union wing under Reynolds moved toward Emmitsburg, with only the III Corps of that wing moving toward Taneytown. Reynolds's marches all exceeded twenty-five miles. The other columns of the army also made marches on June 29 that were long, hot, and challenging, as well. Soldiers in the XII Corps marched during the day until they arrived near Bruceville, Maryland, not far from Emmitsburg and Taneytown. To the south and east, the II Corps, after a delayed start, spent the entire day on the road, arriving in Uniontown late in the day. It was the longest march in that corps' history, thirty-two miles. The Federal V and VI corps brought up the rear of the army. Although pushing throughout the day, the V Corps ended its march south of Liberty, Maryland, while the VI Corps finished its grueling day several miles to the north and east at New Windsor.

Meade also had the cavalry busy as well. Buford's troopers moved to the west and north in search of the Confederate First and Third Corps. Gregg's command headed north and east in search of the Confederate cavalry under Jeb Stuart, with additional orders to guard the flank of the Army of the Potomac. Kilpatrick's newly minted division headed off in search of the Confederate Second Corps.

At the same time, however, new and more accurate intelligence of Confederate dispositions arrived at headquarters, and with it, Meade needed to amend his orders of the previous evening. Meade learned that Confederate forces were at Chambersburg, while further enemy combatants were in Carlisle. These forces were north

Many Union soldiers described St. Joseph's Academy in Emmitsburg, Maryland, in their diaries and letters of late June 1863. (loc)

and west of the advancing columns of the Army of the Potomac. With this intelligence, Meade decided to strengthen the left wing of his army—the wing closest to contact with the Army of Northern Virginia.

Dr. Hubbard, a surgeon in the XI Corps's 17th Connecticut Volunteer Infantry described Emmitsburg in a letter to his wife on June 29:

> *This place 'Emmetsburg [sic]' is a small village of about the size of Fairfield and is pleasantly situated in a valley nearly surrounded by mountains. It is noted as being the center of Catholic influence in this region and contains a Catholic College for boys and a convent for females called the 'Sisterhood of St. Mary.' This last institution is I judge a large one as the buildings connected with it are numerous, very large and elegant being built of very handsome marble.*

The last corps of the left wing, the III Corps, spent most of the day watching as the XII Corps marched past its camp at Taneytown. Finally in the afternoon, the corps moved toward Emmitsburg, a march of only eight miles. The XII Corps was looking to get into Pennsylvania during its march and happily celebrated the feat near noon. One division spent the rest of the day camping at Littlestown, Pennsylvania, while the Second Division, with reports of Confederate activity to the north and east of its position, marched toward Hanover. The final three corps, bringing up the rear of the army also moved little during the day. Although the V and VI corps marched on to Union Mills and Manchester respectively, the II Corps rested in camp all day in Uniontown.

Turn right onto South Seton Avenue, travel 0.4 miles, and take a right onto Main Street. Travel 0.8 miles and take the right exit for Route 15 north towards Gettysburg. Stay on Route 15 north for 2.8 miles and take the right exit for Route 15 Business north towards Gettysburg. Travel 6.2 miles (through the Gettysburg National Military Park) and make a left onto South Washington Street. Stay on South Washington Street for 0.5 miles and make a left onto Route 116 (West Middle Street). Travel 0.6 miles and make a right onto Seminary Ridge. The Seminary Ridge Museum is on your right and parking is on your left.

GPS: N 39 °.832103 W 77 °.244588

STOP 23: SEMINARY RIDGE MUSEUM

Meade ordered his commands to prepare for the advance on the coming day. His orders for June 30 took into consideration all threats by the Confederate army and were in line with his directives from Lincoln and Halleck. Meade placed his commands to be able to march toward or protect Harrisburg, Baltimore, or Washington. With this in mind, the order of march for June 30 inclined the army to the northeast towards York, Pennsylvania. In addition, the lengths of marches were cut significantly. Meade's army was wearing out under the long marches, with their numbers of hours on the hot and dusty roads. In order for the men to be in condition to fight well on the field of battle, Meade wanted to slow the pace of the campaign.

Covering much more ground on June 30 than the Federal infantry was the Federal cavalry. Kilpatrick's division spent the predawn hours of June 30 in Littlestown taking care of his men and mounts and later clashed with Confederate cavalry in Hanover. Gregg's command, meanwhile, reached Westminster by the morning of June 30. He had heard of Stuart's brief occupation of the town, but unsure his intelligence was reliable, Gregg entered the town prepared to fight. After seeing no Confederate activity, he issued orders for the command to remain in Westminster.

At the same time, two brigades from John Buford's division of cavalry reached Gettysburg. "I entered this place to-day at 11 a.m.," Buford wrote to Pleasonton. His troopers met an enthusiastic reception from citizens of the town, happy to know that the Union army was there after their

The Eagle Hotel on the corner of Chambersburg and North Washington Streets in Gettysburg, Pennsylvania, became General Buford's headquarters on June 30 and July 1, 1863. (ecw)

encounter with Early's and Gordon's commands days earlier. Buford at once issued orders for his men to establish vedette posts west, northwest, north, and northeast of Gettysburg. Their job was to screen the approaches to the town itself while gathering as much intelligence on the location, size, and intentions of Confederate units operating in the area. Buford placed significant portions of his men along north-south ridges on the western approach to Gettysburg along the Chambersburg Pike. The ridges, which included Wisler's, McPherson's, and Seminary, were great places to make defensive stands should the need arise. The intelligence Buford received on June 30 told him those positions would be needed. Buford felt sure that the Confederate infantry operating in the area would be back on the Chambersburg Pike the following morning. Buford established his headquarters in the Eagle Hotel on the northwestern end of Gettysburg.

A view of Seminary Ridge and the most iconic building on the campus of the Lutheran Theological Seminary, looking east. This image, taken after the battle, shows the positions that Buford's cavalry and later Federal infantry took on June 30 and July 1, 1863. (loc)

He did not have to wait long before his troopers made contact with elements of the Confederate army.

This concludes the "The Union Response" route. To obtain a tour brochure to the Gettysburg battlefield, visit the Gettysburg National Military Park Visitor Center at 1195 Baltimore Pike, Gettysburg, Pennsylvania 17325. If you are interested, the "Retreat from Gettysburg" chapter begins here at the Seminary Ridge Museum.

Jeb Stuart's Ride

CHAPTER THREE

This route follows Confederate Maj. Gen. Jeb Stuart's cavalry route from Aldie to Gettysburg. It also includes the Loudoun Valley battles of June 17-21, 1863. The entire route is approximately 215 miles.

June 17, 1863, kicked off several days of heated battles between Union and Confederate cavalry. These actions were all part of Maj. Gen. James Ewell Brown "Jeb" Stuart's defense of the Blue Ridge Mountain passes into the Shenandoah Valley, where the Army of Northern Virginia made northward progress with each passing day. General Lee ordered Stuart to protect these gaps and screen against the prying eyes of Federal cavalry operating in the area. Lee needed to maintain the secrecy of his intent, direction of march, purpose, and strength. Stuart established his headquarters in the Loudoun Valley at Middleburg and ordered 2,000 cavalry troopers under the command of Col. Thomas Munford (temporarily commanding Brig. Gen. Fitzhugh Lee's brigade) east towards Aldie, where the fight for the Loudoun Valley and these mountain gaps began.

Munford's men were not the only troopers under Stuart's command. Riding with Stuart's division were five brigades of cavaliers from Maryland, North Carolina, South Carolina, and Virginia, as well as a brigade of horse artillery. In command of these units were brigadiers such as: Wade Hampton, Beverly Robertson, William

The 1st Massachusetts Cavalry Monument at Aldie sits near the stone wall along the road where the Bay Staters met a dreadful carnage. (dw)

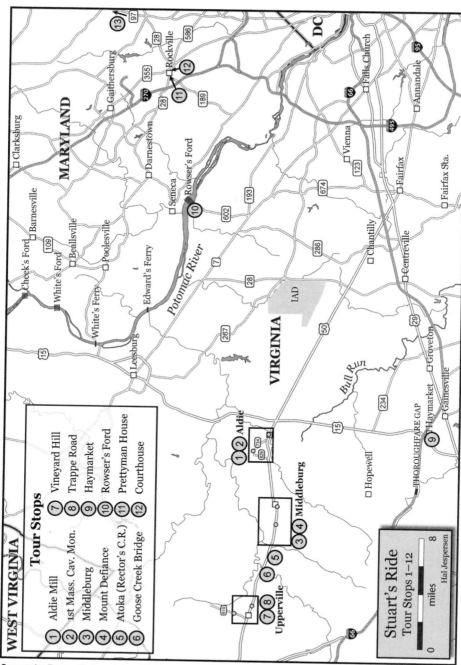

STUART'S RIDE—Ordered to shield the Confederate infantry in the Shenandoah Valley, Stuart's cavalry fought a series of fierce battles in the Loudoun Valley from June 17 – June 21, 1863. Soon after, Stuart received permission from Lee to take a sizeable portion of his cavalry around the Army of the Potomac and reconnect with the Confederate infantry once north of the Mason-Dixon Line. Thus began one of the most debated episodes of the Civil War.

"Grumble" Jones, and Col. John Chambliss. Stuart's division, particularly since Brandy Station, faced a much better opponent than it did in 1861 or 1862. Although the Union cavalry experienced command shake-ups over the coming weeks during the Gettysburg campaign, the cavalry corps had numerous able officers. Commanding these Federal cavalry brigades were colonels William Gamble, Thomas Devin, John Taylor, and John Gregg. Later promoted to brigadier-generals were Wesley Merritt, George Custer, and Elon Farnsworth. Taking overall command of these brigades were division commanders John Buford, David Gregg, and towards the end of June 1863, Judson Kilpatrick.

Begin the "Jeb Stuart's Ride" Tour at Aldie Mill Historic Park located at 39401 John Mosby Hwy, Aldie, Virginia 20105. The village of Aldie, founded by Charles Fenton Mercer, sits in the Aldie Gap in the Bull Run Mountains. In June 1863, it was a strategic location for the Confederate cavalry attempting to screen Lee's infantry as well as for the Federal cavalry attempting to locate Lee and determine what he was up to.

Richmond native and Virginia Military Institute graduate Col. Thomas Munford temporarily led Brig. Gen. Fitzhugh Lee's brigade during the Gettysburg campaign. (phocw)

GPS: N 38° .975468 W 77° .641416

STOP 1: BATTLE OF ALDIE: ALDIE MILL

Two macadamized turnpikes—the latest in road technology, which afforded faster, easier, and more efficient movement for both civilians and the military—led west from Aldie to two mountain gaps, Ashby and Snickers. It was critical for Confederate cavalry to protect it. Generals Hooker and Pleasonton also recognized the importance of Aldie and the roads that led westward from the town. To confirm reports of Lee's movements in the Valley, the two Union generals realized they had to penetrate the gaps for a

Ashby's Gap, located in the Blue Ridge Mountains, became important in the 1800s because a vital turnpike connecting the Shenandoah Valley and Alexandria ran through the gap. This wartime sketch of Ashby's Gap was drawn by Alfred Waud. (loc)

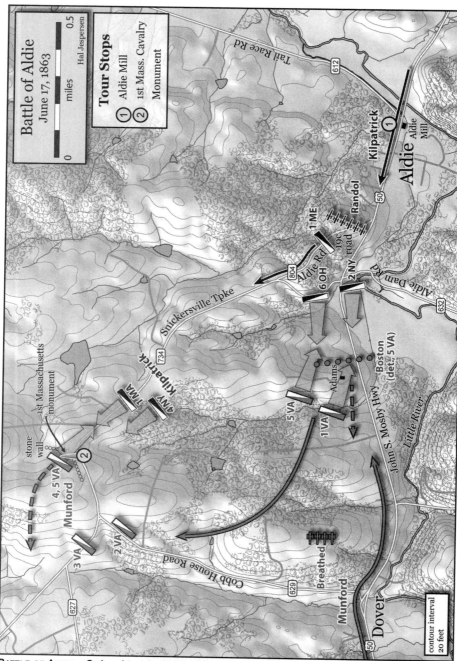

BATTLE OF ALDIE— Ordered to take his Federal cavalry west towards the Blue Ridge Mountains to gather information on Lee's whereabouts and intentions, Kilpatrick first encounters Confederate cavalry at Aldie. The Confederates were forced to cover both the Ashby Gap Turnpike and Snickersville Turnpike, since both led to important gaps in the Blue Ridge Mountains. After a day of sharp fighting, the Confederates pulled back to Middleburg due to reports of Federal cavalry in their rear.

look into the Valley itself. They sent Brig. Gen. Judson Kilpatrick's 1,200-man cavalry brigade.

About 2:30 p.m. on June 17, elements of Munford's and Kilpatrick's brigades clashed in Aldie. The fighting grew in size as the noise of the battle drew more Confederate cavalry to the scene. With more Federal cavalry arriving, the Confederates pulled back to the hills just west of the town.

Carefully turn left out of the parking area onto Route 50 West (John S. Mosby Highway), drive 0.6 miles and make a right onto Route 734 (Snickersville Turnpike). You will drive through the historic village of Aldie, which contains many wartime buildings. Once you make the turn onto Route 734, you will be following the route of the Union attack under Kilpatrick against the 2nd and 3rd Virginia Cavalry. In 1.2 miles at the intersection with Oatlands Road, you will come to the Furr House and, soon, a sharp bend in the road. At the bend, there is a small pull-off on the right side in front of the 1st Massachusetts Cavalry Monument.

GPS: N 38° .991988 W 77° .663921

STOP 2: BATTLE OF ALDIE: 1ST MASSACHUSETTS CAVALRY MONUMENT

While fighting took place along Ashby's Gap Turnpike (modern day Route 50), more of Kilpatrick's Federal cavalry arrived within supporting distance. One unit, the 1st Massachusetts Cavalry, was ordered northwestward along the Snickersville Turnpike. Kilpatrick believed this area and road to be devoid of Confederate defenders; he could not have been more wrong. The commander of the 1st Massachusetts, Lt. Col. Greely Curtis, sent a small detachment ahead to reconnoiter the road. He ran into a small Confederate force and moved them out of the way. Unfortunately for the Bay Staters, they were not able to see the main Confederate line around the Furr House. As the rest of the regiment reached the vicinity of the Furr farm, the dismounted Confederate cavalry, well protected and defended by tall stone walls, unleashed a furious fire into the squadron. It was a devastating blow. Further attacks against the strong Confederate position ensued across the Furr property; none succeeded.

The fight here was not over, though. More Confederate troopers from the 2nd, 3rd, 4th, and 5th Virginia Cavalry arrived on the scene, as well as the 1st Maine Cavalry.

American Civil War sketch artist Alfred Waud sketched this piece, "1st Maine Cavalry Skirmishing," during the several days of continuous cavalry combat at Aldie, Middleburg, and Upperville. The sketch was published in *Harper's Weekly* **on September 5, 1863.** (loc)

The Confederates pushed southward down the pike in a fierce fight, but their gallantry, bravery, and eagerness were not enough to win the day. These units pulled back to the Furr property and its surrounding fields and walls. With further reinforcements, Union cavalry probed down the pike yet again. Although the Virginians were able to fight off further Federal attempts at their position, reports of Federal cavalry in their rear near Middleburg compelled Stuart to call the Confederate cavalry back to Middleburg.

Return to Route 734 and retrace your route back to Route 50 (be careful as this portion of the road can be busy and is a blind spot). Once you reach Route 50, turn right and then you will immediately see a Civil War Trails sign on the right. Pull over and read the signs. In the fields behind the sign, the initial fighting took place between the 2nd and 5th Virginia Cavalry and the 2nd, 4th New York and 6th Ohio Cavalry. Continue west on Route 50. You will pass "Briar Patch" on the right, which was the Adams House during the battle. The ridge beyond was the location of Breathed's artillery. From the Civil War Trails marker, drive 4.1 miles to the village of Middleburg. Take notice of the beautiful landscape of this area; many of these farms date back to the nineteenth-century. Once you enter Middleburg, drive 0.6 miles and take a left onto Route 626 (The Plains Road). As you drive through town, at the lone stop light, is the Red Fox Inn on your right, one of the oldest taverns in the region. Stuart used this building for a time as his headquarters during the battle at Aldie. Once you make the left to Route 626, make a right into the parking lot of the National Sporting Library and Museum. The Civil War Trails marker is located to the left in the parking lot. Be sure to visit the Civil War Horse and Mule Memorial in front of the museum.

GPS: N 38° .966493 W 77° .738752

STOP 3: MIDDLEBURG

During the morning hours of June 17, while fighting at Aldie was taking place five miles to the east, a detached Federal cavalry unit rode for the rear of Stuart's line. The column arrived at its destination in Middleburg by late afternoon. The unit that had participated on this daring ride was the 1st Rhode Island Cavalry led by Col. Alfred N. A. Duffié. His 300 men surprised Stuart and his staff and forced the cavalier to relocate his headquarters to Rector's Crossroads, four miles to the west. The Rhode Islanders were ordered to barricade the town, but Duffié realized it would be a hard fight to maintain his gains. As the evening descended on the town, Stuart ordered two regiments, the 4th and 5th North Carolina Cavalry, to ride back to Middleburg and retake the town. Also approaching Middleburg at Stuart's orders was Chambliss's command. The fight that erupted late on June 17 was fierce, but Duffié found himself severely outnumbered and out matched. Only with darkness did the Federals have a respite from Confederate attacks.. Darkness brought an end to the battle. The following morning, June 18, Confederate cavalry were in pursuit of the Rhode Islanders along the Plains Road. Duffié ordered his men to flee and make their escape on their own. Confederates caught up with many of them near Burnt Mill Run, capturing more than 200 men, minus Duffié who made his escape southeastward over the Bull Run Mountains at Hopewell Gap.

A West Point graduate, Col. John R. Chambliss left the military for a time before the American Civil War. Soon, however, he used his military education and worked as an aide-de-camp for Virginia Governor Henry A. Wise. When the war began, Chambliss remained loyal to his native state and rose through the ranks of the cavalry. During the Gettysburg campaign, his men saw hard service. (loc)

If you are interested in driving the road where the running battle between Chambliss and Duffié took place, take a right out of the parking lot. It is approximately 2 miles to Burnt Mill Run. Many of the stone walls are original and were used by both sides.

To continue on the main tour, take a left out of the parking lot and return to Route 50 West (West Washington Street). Take a left onto Washington Street and travel 1.3 miles and take a left (the first turn AFTER Zulla Road). Be careful, as the four-

Heros von Borcke was wounded along this treeline during the battle of Middleburg. (dw)

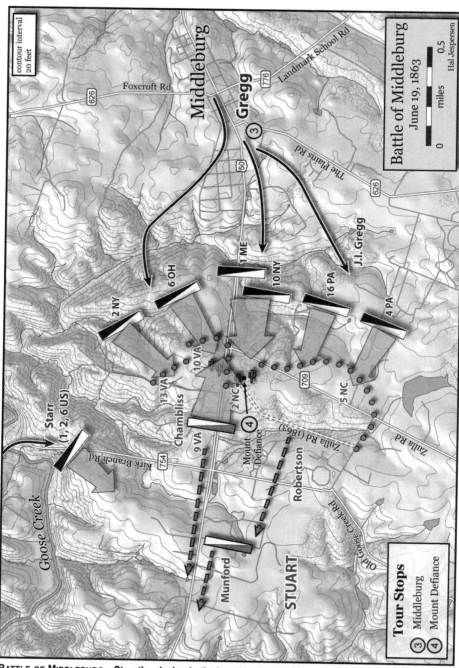

BATTLE OF MIDDLEBURG—Stuart's mission in the Loudoun Valley was to keep the Federal cavalry from gaining information about Lee's infantry. Therefore, he did not have to defeat the Federal cavalry; he just had to delay them and thwart their approach to the mountain gaps. He devised a strategy to use the various hills along the Ashby Gap Turnpike as defensive positions. Here on a low rise west of Middleburg, Stuart's cavalry centered their defense around a place called Mount Defiance. After heavy fighting, the Federals flanked the Confederate position, forcing the Confederates to withdraw to the next defensible position near Rector's Crossroads.

lane highway can be very busy. When you turn into the median, look carefully to your right for oncoming traffic, then you will go straight across the eastbound lanes into the driveway for Mount Defiance. This property is now preserved by NOVA Parks. As of 2016, there is not a designated parking area, but pull up in the driveway and the Civil War Trails marker is ahead on your left. More interpretive markers are now in the planning stages. The house and buildings here are private residences, so please respect their privacy.

GPS: N 38° .967589 77° .762769

STOP 4: BATTLE OF MIDDLEBURG: MOUNT DEFIANCE

Colonel J. Irvin Gregg's four regiments and Brig. Gen. Kilpatrick's two regiments of Federal cavalry quickly drove Confederate pickets from Middleburg on the morning of June 19. Gregg deployed his men south of Ashby's Gap Turnpike where they encountered five Confederate cavalry units from Gen. Robertson and Col. Chambliss' commands. The area, known as Mount Defiance, is a low north-south ridge west of Middleburg. Mount Defiance was the scene of severe hand-to-hand fighting throughout the day. Some of the heaviest fighting occurred along the turnpike itself and near a blacksmith shop (which still stands on the property at Mt. Defiance). Defending this position was Chambliss' command supported by Capt. William McGregor's horse artillery. Mounted Federal troopers from New York, Maine, Ohio, and Pennsylvania assaulted the gray horsemen throughout the day. The continual pressure on this sector of the Confederate line led Chambliss and Robertson's command to give ground.

With Confederate lines staggering and increased pressure on the front and flank from Union troopers, Stuart and his Prussian-born assistant adjutant and

"Explosion of a rebel limber at the battle near Middleburg June 21st" by Alfred Waud. (loc)

The blacksmith shop at Mount Defiance was the scene of fierce fighting during the battle of Middleburg. (dw)

inspector general, Maj. Johann August Heinrich Heros von Borcke, rode to the ground west of the blacksmith shop to steady the men. The position was hot, and von Borcke received a minor wound when a bullet grazed his leg. Moments later, another bullet pierced his throat. Captain William Blackford and Lt. Frank Robertson rushed to the wounded officer. Blackford later recalled the scene: "I was at my wits' end to know how we were to throw our friend's body, weighing two hundred and fifty pounds, across the rearing, plunging charger. . . ." The Prussian was first taken to Upperville to recover from his wound before being transferred to Richmond. Although he survived, it ended his military field career. As more Union troopers arrived from the north on Stuart's flank, the general established a secondary position farther west. From there, troopers of Chambliss's command attacked these Federals from Buford's command at Battle Knoll but with little success. At the end of a long day of fighting, the strategic cavalry situation in the area remained stalemated.

Turn around and exit the way you came in. Carefully cross over to the median and take a left onto Route 50 west (John S. Mosby Highway). This is a dangerous intersection, so please use extreme caution. Travel 2.5 miles and make a left onto Route 828 (Atoka Road). Immediately to your left is a parking area for a Civil War Trails sign.

GPS: N 38° .975608 W 77° .807961

STOP 5: ATOKA (RECTOR'S CROSSROADS)

Col. John Irvin Gregg, a Mexican War veteran, commanded a brigade of Federal cavalry in a division commanded by his cousin, David Gregg, during the Gettysburg campaign. (ch)

The village of Atoka was known as Rector's Crossroads during the war. By June 20, 1863, more Confederate cavalry arrived in the area. Both Grumble Jones's and Wade Hampton's brigades augmented Stuart's forces along Ashby's Gap Turnpike towards Upperville. This increase in Confederate manpower led Pleasonton to believe that not only did he face a sizeable cavalry foe in his front, but that the Confederate troopers were supported by mounted infantry. Pleasonton requested infantry supports for his troopers from Hooker. Hooker sent a division from the V Corps under the command of Brig. Gen. James Barnes towards Middleburg. The following day, June 21, Col. Strong Vincent's brigade—consisting of the 16th Michigan, 44th New York, 83rd Pennsylvania and the 20th Maine arrived. Pleasonton suggested a plan that placed the infantry brigade south of the turnpike in support of Gregg's troopers on the pike itself, while Buford's troopers once again rode north in an effort to get on the flank and in the rear of Stuart's position. Pleasanton's plan went into action early that morning.

The battle quickly heated up as Union and Confederate artillery duelled. During the bombardment, Union forces moved forward. Vincent's brigade south of the pike applied immense pressure on the Confederate right flank and rear while Kilpatrick's men did the same on the Confederate left near Battle Knoll. Stuart's position between Upperville to his rear and Middleburg to his front was giving ground. As the Confederates succumbed to the pressure, Stuart had a problem. Immediately to his rear was Cromwell's Run and one narrow stone bridge that spanned it. Captain Hart's three remaining Confederate guns were ordered to cover the retreat of the gray cavaliers. Hart was successful, and Stuart's troopers continued their ride westward.

Located here is the Rector House, where on June 10, 1863, Maj. John S. Mosby formed his famed 43rd Virginia Cavalry Battalion (Mosby's Rangers). Mosby provided local intelligence and scouting for Stuart during June 1863. After the fighting in the region ended, Stuart set up his headquarters here on June 22, and with the help of Mosby, planned his controversial route to Pennsylvania. Today the building serves as the headquarters of the Mosby Heritage Area Association.

Return to Route 50 (John S. Mosby Highway), and turn left. Travel 0.9 miles and make a right onto Route 832 (Lemmons Bottom Road). To the right there will be a gravel drive that circles toward the parking area for a Civil War Trails sign. Be sure to walk to the actual bridge as well. This

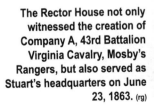

The Rector House not only witnessed the creation of Company A, 43rd Battalion Virginia Cavalry, Mosby's Rangers, but also served as Stuart's headquarters on June 23, 1863. (rg)

beautiful bridge was built in 1802 as part of the turnpike that led from Aldie to Winchester.

GPS: N 38° .981883 W 77° .820998

STOP 6: GOOSE CREEK BRIDGE

You are now looking at the historic Goose Creek Bridge, a local landmark for over 200 years. The bridge was one of the largest along the Ashby's Gap Turnpike. Stuart planned on using the creek and the high ridge to the west as a defensive position to continue to delay the Federal advance.

To provide enough time for the Confederate troopers and artillery to get across the creek, as well as establish a strong position on its western ridges, Stuart ordered one of Wade Hampton's units to ride eastward on the pike, take a position, and slow the Union advance. Tapped for the assignment was the 1st South Carolina Cavalry. Colonel John Black, commanding the regiment, reached Rector's Crossroads; here he dismounted 200 of his men and left the rest of the unit mounted to the rear. Once Stuart's new position was prepared, he ordered the Carolinians to the west side of the creek and ordered them to rejoin the rest of Hampton's brigade.

Not long after the 1st South Carolina crossed over the bridge, Kilpatrick's troopers and Vincent's infantry arrived. The heights on the west side of Goose Creek were impressive, and, coupled with Stuart's well-laid position, the Federal advance ground to a halt. Kilpatrick did not desire to send his men forward to attack such a strong position and looked for tactical input from Pleasonton. While these two generals determined what to do next, the second artillery duel of the day opened. In the meantime, Stuart sent orders to Chambliss and Jones to meet at Upperville. The commanding general knew that, despite a strong defense at Goose Creek, it was only a matter of time before he would be forced to abandon the line. Upperville was his last line of defense before Ashby's Gap and panoramic views of Lee's army.

While the Confederate cavalry was in motion, Pleasonton made a decision. He determined that Goose Creek Bridge was the key to the Confederate tactical position and ordered Kilpatrick to take it. Kilpatrick

Goose Creek Bridge, built circa 1810, is the largest stone turnpike bridge in northern Virginia. Its use to take people across the creek came to an end when U.S. Route 50 was constructed. (dw)

LEFT: Brig. Gen. James Barnes, a West Point graduate from the same class as Robert E. Lee, gained recognition for his ability to lead his command at the battle of Fredericksburg. By June 1863, he commanded a division in the V Corps. (gnmp)

RIGHT: Col. Strong Vincent commanded a brigade destined for fame at Little Round Top. The regiments under his command supported Federal cavalry several times during the ongoing cavalry engagements in mid-June 1863, including at Goose Creek Bridge. (loc)

first sent the 4th New York Cavalry headlong against the bridge itself. Although he only sent one company of the regiment, it was still enough to discover that a direct assault on the span was not possible. Kilpatrick, despite the result of the first assault, quickly organized a second attack. This time, however, he sent the 2nd New York and 6th Ohio Cavalry in addition to the 16th Michigan Infantry from Vincent's brigade directly toward the bridge to occupy the attention of the Southern defenders, while other elements of the two commands, the 83rd Pennsylvania Infantry and the 4th New York Cavalry, attacked and forded the creek where they could. The new assault was too much for the Confederate defenders, and for the second time on June 21, Stuart was forced to pull his command back.

Return to Route 50 (John S. Mosby Highway) and make a right. Travel 2.8 miles and make a left into a gravel drive that leads to a parking area for a baseball field. Two Civil War Trails markers will be to your left, facing east (the battle area around Vineyard Hill).

GPS: N 38° .990542 W 77° .872196

STOP 7: BATTLE OF UPPERVILLE: VINEYARD HILL

By the afternoon of June 21, 1863, the Confederate cavalry had been in an ongoing, fighting withdrawal. After Stuart ordered his men to retire from their Goose Creek Bridge position to the east, his command headed toward Upperville, a concentration point and last line of defense. The hills around Upperville were the last defensive positions before Ashby's Gap. During

View from Vineyard Hill in Upperville, Virginia. The Federal cavalry attacked across the fields in the distance. (dw)

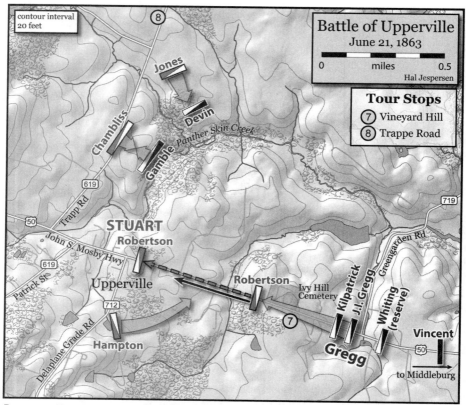

BATTLE OF UPPERVILLE—The hills around Upperville presented the last location in the Loudoun Valley where Stuart could delay the Federal cavalry from gaining access to Ashby Gap. Stuart's cavalry was divided by the village of Upperville, and both wings saw strong attacks by Federal cavalry. With heavy action both at Ivy Hill and Trappe Road, Stuart was forced to pull his men back towards Paris at the base of Ashby's Gap.

the occupation of the Goose Creek line, Stuart ordered Chambliss's and Jones's brigades to concentrate near the Virginia town. By the late afternoon, the Confederates were under attack.

The fight at Upperville quickly became the largest battle between the cavalry forces since the fight at Brandy Station on June 9. At Vineyard Hill, 10,000 cavalry troopers engaged in hand-to-hand fighting, brandishing pistols and sabers. Stuart selected this position because of its clear view of the road and the numerous stone walls behind which his men could fight dismounted, offering a distinct advantage. The Confederate horsemen soon were under attack by three brigades of Union cavalry. Kilpatrick's brigade was the first into action. The young, impetuous commander did not want the United States

"Battle near Upperville. Ashbys Gap in Distance," sketched by Alfred Waud on June 21, 1863. (loc)

Regulars to reach Upperville first, and in his haste, ordered his men forward in an attack unsupported. The assault failed with disastrous results. The U.S. Regular cavalry did not fare any better, however. Their assaults were uncoordinated and piecemeal. Stuart and his men repelled each subsequent assault, but each attack took its toll on his men, ammunition, and energy.

Return to Route 50 (John S. Mosby Highway) and make a left. Driving 1 mile, you will pass through the village of Upperville. Make a right onto Route 619 (Trappe Road) and travel 1 mile to a Civil War Trails marker on the left side of the road.

GPS: N 39° .008774 W 77° .882385

STOP 8: BATTLE OF UPPERVILLE: TRAPPE ROAD

By the late afternoon of June 21, Gamble's and Devin's brigades began their assaults against the Southern troopers here, over the Kirkby and Ayrshire properties. In all, nearly 6,000 soldiers, including the horse artillery, were thrown into the fight, which became perilous for the Confederate horsemen. In order to pull out of their position along the Trappe Road and fall back to Ashby's Gap, they had to make a break to the turnpike. As they faced mounting pressure in their front, the fight two miles to their southeast, at Vineyard Hill, decided the two brigades' fate.

When Stuart found out about Jones's and Chambliss's successful escape south along the Trappe Road to Ashby's Gap Turnpike and west towards Paris— as well as the escape of the supply wagons—he ordered Robertson's and Hampton's brigades to pull out of their position at Vineyard Hill. Robertson's men were already pulling back in the face of Kilpatrick's attack (as well as the presence of Buford on their northern flank). These men

Col. Thomas C. Devin, a painter by trade before the war, had limited militia experience in his native state of New York. Devin's hard-hitting brigade was relied upon time and again by division commander John Buford. (loc)

came under fire yet again that afternoon. The 1st Maine Cavalry rode headlong into the Confederate position, but Robertson's men gave them a warm welcome. The Mainers fell back after a hot, close fight. Support was on the way, though: the 2nd New York, supported by the 4th and 16th Pennsylvania Cavalry. With the added weight of the Federal reinforcements, Robertson's men retired westward along Ashby's Gap Turnpike and to the Blue Ridge Mountains.

Darkness fell by the time Stuart's command arrived at the gap and mountains. The flamboyant general hoped the gathering night would dissuade any further Federal cavalry pursuit of his command. Lee, however, did not rely on the darkness and sent McLaws's division of Longstreet's Corps from the west to further protect the pass from the prying eyes of Union cavalry. The Confederate commands were relieved. Pleasonton did not push farther that evening or press the issue at the gap. Later that evening, Pleasonton sent a communiqué to Hooker with information gathered during the day and the subsequent fight. He notified Hooker that Lee's army was not in Loudoun Valley and that he would return to Aldie the following morning. Pleasonton, however, could *not* help Hooker identify where the Army of Northern Virginia *was* located.

On the night of June 21, while the rest of the Federal cavalry headed to Aldie, Buford sent scouts to the nearby mountain range. There, the scouts noticed the campfires of McLaws's division and Buford quickly sent the information to Hooker—but Hooker took three more days to move his army in reaction to the report.

Although Buford's report was accurate—and although the vital information was largely ignored, the effort was costly. A week's worth of fighting, fatigued mounts, low supplies, and high casualties marked both sides. The battles at Aldie, Middleburg, and Upperville cost Stuart's troopers nearly 600 men in casualties, while Pleasonton's riders lost even more, more than 900 men in all. Had the cost of these lives been worth the intelligence gained, considering Hooker's reaction to it?

Return the way you came to Route 50. Just left (east) of the intersection of Trappe Road and Route 50 is a pull-off with two Civil War Trails markers. Feel free to pull off and read the markers. Both relate to the Gettysburg campaign. Take

Route 50 west (a right from Trappe Road) for 3.1 miles towards the Blue Ridge Mountains. Take a left onto Route 17 south (Winchester Road). If you drive straight, you will go through the Blue Ridge Mountains at Ashby's Gap, one of the gaps that Stuart was fighting so hard to keep out of Federal hands.

Travel Route 17 south for 8 miles and take Interstate 66 east (Route 17 will merge onto Interstate 66). Stay on Interstate 66 east for 16.3 miles and take Exit 40 onto Route 15 south. Then take Route 55 east (Washington Street) and travel 0.4 miles to the Haymarket Museum on the right. There are two Civil War Trails markers on the east side of the museum from the parking lot.

GPS: N 38° .812465 W 77° .637491

STOP 9: HAYMARKET

Perhaps the most excitement for Stuart's command following the engagements at Aldie, Middleburg, and Upperville began at 1:00 a.m. on June 25, 1863, when Stuart led his brigades through Glasscock's Gap and towards Haymarket, Virginia. Stuart's troopers, numbering more than 5,000, saw little Federal activity until they reached the outskirts of Haymarket. "As we neared Hay Market," Stuart recalled, "we found that Hancock's corps was *en route* through Hay Market for Gum Springs, his infantry well distributed through his trains." Ever the fighter, Stuart quickly reconnoitered the ground, found a position on which to place his artillery, and opened on the Federal II Corps. The artillery barrage had the effect of "scattering men, wagons, and [sent] horses in wild confusion." The fire "had disabled one of the enemy's caissons, which he abandoned, and compelled him to advance in order of battle to compel us to desist."

Stuart's next steps after this encounter have become the stuff of legend and controversy.

Lee and Longstreet advised that if Stuart found his way blocked, his proposed ride around the Army of the Potomac should be scrapped and he

The small town of Buckland in Prince William County, Virginia, would again play host to Stuart's cavalry in the fall of 1863 at the battle of Buckland Mills. (dw)

should report back to the Army of Northern Virginia. Intelligence Stuart gathered from his engagement with the II Corps and other sources, indicated that his way through the Army of the Potomac was indeed blocked. Yet, Stuart decided not to return to the army; rather, he readjusted his route further to the south and east. This plan took Stuart and three brigades of cavalry even further from the Army of Northern Virginia. It required a longer time on the march to get around the Federal army and, at the very least, risked the exhaustion of men and mounts in the meantime. Stuart did leave Lee with the brigades of Jones, Jenkins and Robertson.

For the rest of June 25, Stuart grazed "our horses, the only forage procurable in the country," and moved toward Buckland. In his campaign report, Stuart laid out his next step: "To carry out my original design of passing west of Centreville, would have involved so much detentions, on account of the presence of the enemy that I determined to cross Bull Run lower down, and strike through Fairfax for the Potomac the next day. The sequel shows this to have been the only practicable course."

The following day, Stuart continued on this much longer route around the Federal army. "We marched through Brentsville to the vicinity of Wolf Run Shoals," wrote Stuart, but "had to halt again in order to graze our horses, which hard marching without grain was fast breaking down" (the "Union Advance" chapter has a stop for Wolf Run Shoals). However, Stuart had finally broken free of Federal entanglements when he noted on the 26th, "We met no enemy to-day."

Turn left onto Route 55 (Washington Street), then take a right onto Route 15 north (James Monroe Highway). Take the exit for Interstate 66 east, travel 14.4 miles, and take Exit 55B—Route 286 north (Fairfax County Parkway). Travel 12.3 miles and take Route 7 east (Leesburg Pike). Continue on Route 7 for 1 mile then make a left onto Route 193 (Georgetown Pike), then take your immediate left onto Route 602 (Seneca Road). Travel 3.7 miles, and the road will end in a parking lot. At the end of the parking lot there is a trailhead with two Civil War interpretive markers. If you have time, there is a trail that follows an old road trace that will take you down to the location of the wartime Rowser's Ford (approximately 0.7 miles).

GPS: N 39° .051633 W 77° .334104

STOP 10: ROWSER'S FORD

Stuart's troopers faced serious obstacles on June 27. Early in the day, Stuart detached various commands from his division for specific assignments. First, Fitz Lee's brigade was ordered to Burke's Station before rejoining the command at Fairfax Station. Following Lee's return and "[a]fter a halt of a few hours to rest and refresh the command," Stuart ordered his entire command to Dranesville. Once there, he detached Gen. Hampton's brigade to move for Rowser's Ford on the Potomac River. During this time, Stuart learned that the Army of the Potomac was moving north and leaving Virginia.

Hampton found the ford to be swollen nearly two feet higher than normal from recent rains. Although he was able to get his troopers across the river using the ford, Hampton sent word back to Stuart that moving the artillery across the ford was impossible. Stuart immediately looked for other crossing sites for the command's artillery and troopers, but found none suitable. "I, however, determined not to give it up without trial," wrote Stuart, and "in spite of the difficulties, to all appearances insuperable, indomitable energy and resolute determination triumphed; every piece was brought safely over, and the entire command in bivouac on Maryland soil." Stuart's column did not cross into Maryland without leaving their mark on the C&O Canal, however. His troopers captured numerous boats on the canal, along with Federal soldiers and supplies, in addition to damaging locks on the canal itself. Later it took nearly three days to repair the damage caused by Stuart's cavalry.

The trip to the next tour stop in Rockville, Maryland, will travel through areas that are susceptible to heavy traffic. It will take you approximately 45 minutes to reach the next stop. Please be cognizant of traffic and busy roads.

Retrace your route down Route 602 (Seneca Road) for 3.6

This modern image shows Lock 24 near Rowser's Ford. Stuart's men caused significant destruction to the lock houses and canals in the area of their crossing. (dw)

A view looking towards Rowser's Ford. Here, Stuart's cavalry crossed the Potomac River into Maryland during their controversial ride. (dw)

miles and make a left onto Route 193 (Georgetown Pike). Travel 9.3 miles and take a left onto Interstate 495 north (Inner Loop). Remain on Interstate 495 for 4.6 miles and take the left exit ramp for Interstate 270 north. Stay on Interstate 270 for 4.4 miles and take Exit 5—Route 189 north (follow right exit ramp). Once on Route 189, immediately get in the left turn lane to make a left onto Great Falls Road. In 0.8 miles, turn right onto West Jefferson Street. The Prettyman House and Civil War Trails marker is on the right side of the street, just after the intersection with South Van Buren Street.

GPS: N 39° .083111 W 77° .156205

STOP 11: ROCKVILLE: PRETTYMAN HOUSE

Stuart's command was back in the saddle on June 28. The men had started their crossing of the Potomac River the night before and, nearing 3:00 a.m. on June 28, the entire command finally entered Maryland. Stuart's brigadiers wasted no time in looking for the spoils of war. "General Hampton encountered small parties of the enemy, which, with a number of wagons and teams, he captured," wrote Stuart in his post-campaign report. W.H.F. Lee's command engaged elements of the 2nd New York Cavalry during the day, and, by the day's end, "Rockville was speedily taken possession of" as well. While the Confederate cavalry was in Rockville, many of its enslaved inhabitants, according to one Rockville resident, "cleared out," using the chaos and excitement of the Confederate occupation to slip away. And, chaos it was. Stuart ordered his 5,000 men to

The Prettyman house in Rockville, Maryland, was completed in 1842. The current home reflects changes made after the Civil War in the 1870s and remained in the Prettyman family until the 1960s. (dw)

destroy telegraph lines, collect citizens disloyal to the Confederacy and place them under arrest, and find food and forage for his men and mounts in the surrounding countryside. Through the chaos, Stuart's troopers received a warm reception by many citizens sympathetic to their cause.

Meanwhile, on the other side of Rockville, Stuart paused at the home of E. Barrett Prettyman. The local hosted Stuart while the cavalier played with the educator's youngest child, Forest. Stuart did not have long to dote. While at the Prettyman house, he received intelligence of a Federal wagon train laden with supplies heading down the Rockville Pike towards the town of Frederick, where much of the Army of the Potomac had concentrated on June 28. He quickly issued orders for Chambliss's command to intercept the wagon train. The orders proved to be successful and the capture immense. Moments later, Stuart was back on his mount and heading for Rockville's courthouse to check on his other commands and their "work" in the town.

Continue east on West Jefferson Street two blocks and make a left onto South Washington Street. Then make a right onto West Montgomery Avenue. The courthouse square will be to your right. The Civil War Trails markers is on your right in the courthouse square along the sidewalk on Maryland Avenue.

GPS: N 39° .083754 W 77° .151094

The Confederate monument located next to the Courthouse in Rockville, Maryland, was vandalized in the summer of 2015. This photo was taken just days earlier. (dw)

STOP 12: ROCKVILLE: COURTHOUSE

Those citizens arrested by Stuart's troopers, including Provost Marshall Mortimer Moulden and Postmaster Thomas Bailey, were taken to the courthouse and held there throughout June 28. Later that evening, the Confederate column moved out, taking with them a significant number of prisoners and loot. In all, Stuart's command had 400 prisoners consisting of loyalist citizens of Rockville, 150 United States Colored Troops with their white officers from Edwards Ferry, and numerous African Americans from surrounding farms. The men in Stuart's command also took $40,000 in soldiers' wages from the United States Quartermaster's store, 900 mules, and 125 wagons full of supplies, including oats and whiskey. In all, June 28 proved fruitful for Stuart's command. The fruits of the troopers' work, however, proved to be a bane for the command because it slowed the pace of their advance. With these encumbrances, could Stuart effectively continue his ride?

Finally completed in 1891, the Red Brick Courthouse in Rockville, Maryland, is the oldest courthouse in Montgomery County, Maryland. (dw)

The next driving route will take you through congested areas, so please be cognizant of traffic. Take Maryland Avenue north one block and make a right onto East Middle Lane. Drive 0.3 miles (East Middle Lane will become Park Road) and take a right onto South Stonestreet Avenue. Drive 0.2 miles and make a left onto Baltimore Road. Travel Baltimore Road for 0.4 miles and make

The Brookeville Academy in Brookeville, Maryland, witnessed Stuart's arrival in late June 1863. It was also in Brookeville that Stuart paroled a large number of Federal and civilian prisoners captured in and around Rockville. (dw)

Maj. James C. Duane, a West Point graduate and later instructor of engineering at the academy, served as an engineer with the Army of the Potomac. Duane, as well as Capt. Nathaniel Michler, were captured by Stuart's cavalry and later paroled when the Confederate column paused at Brookeville. (loc)

a left onto Route 28 (First Street). First Street will become Norbeck Road. Continue for 3.7 miles to the intersection with Route 97. Make a left onto Route 97 (Georgia Avenue), and travel 5 miles to the town of Brookeville. The Civil War Trails marker is on Georgia Avenue along the sidewalk in front of the Brookeville Academy.

GPS: N 39° .180446 W 77° .058635

STOP 13: BROOKEVILLE

A large majority of Stuart's command left Rockville late in the afternoon and early evening of June 28, 1863, via the Baltimore Road. By nightfall, elements of the 5,000-man column—as well as the spoils Stuart had captured—arrived in Brookeville. Two captured Union officers, Maj. James C. Duane, an engineer with the Army of the Potomac, and Capt. Nathaniel Michler, U.S. Army Corps of Engineers, "urgently solicited" Stuart to parole those prisoners he had captured. He consented. Official paroles, however, took an immense amount of time, and it further delayed his ride. H. B. McClellan saw this delay as a direct result of "Stuart's humanity towards his prisoners." McClellan believed, however, that the parole was "a useless task; for the Federal authorities refused to acknowledge the parole, and returned officers and men immediately to duty." Those civilians who were taken prisoner had a long walk back to Rockville and its environs over the course of the next day.

Continue on Route 97 (Georgia Avenue), make a left turn at the next intersection to stay on Route 97. Travel 10.6 miles on Route 97 (Georgia Avenue), then pull into the Park and Ride lot on the right side after the intersection of Route 97 and Route 144 (Frederick Road). There are two Civil War Trails markers in the parking lot.

GPS: N 39° .320990 W 77° .019138

STOP 14: COOKSVILLE

After hours spent in Brookeville paroling their prisoners, the Confederate troopers pushed on. During the predawn hours of June 29, the column reached the outskirts of Cooksville. Upon their arrival, advance elements of the column were startled as they ran into Union pickets. These Federal soldiers were part of Capt. R. E. Duvall's Company A, Purnell Legion, Maryland Cavalry, which had camped on the National Road along with two cannon of Capt. W. D. Rank's Battery H, 3rd Pennsylvania Artillery the previous evening. The Federal cavalry commander was responsible for escorting the guns to a viaduct along the B&O Railroad to be used for the railroad's defense. After Duvall's pickets were driven in, he sent Sgt. Andrew Duncan and Pvt. Jonathan Norris to Frederick, site of the Army of the Potomac's concentration, to alert new army commander, General Meade, of Stuart's cavalry operating in the area. Duvall was able to get the rest of his command and the guns he was ordered to protect out of Cooksville with only the loss of several horses and accouterments.

Like James Duane, Capt. Nathaniel Michler was a West Point-trained and career military engineer before the war. He served with the armies of Ohio and Cumberland before being transferred to the Army of the Potomac at the request of Joe Hooker. (loc)

Continue north on Route 97 for 1.1 miles and make a right onto Old Frederick Road. Travel 0.3 miles and continue straight onto Forsythe Road for another 2.9 miles. Make a left onto Route 851 (West Friendship Road). Travel 0.2 miles (crossing the modern railroad tracks of the wartime B&O Railroad). A Civil War Trails marker stands on the right side of the road near the intersection of Main Street and A Street.

GPS: N 39° .364454 W 76° .968992

STOP 15: SYKESVILLE

Stuart sent Fitzhugh Lee's brigade north to the B&O Railroad at Hood's Mill (two miles southwest of here). Lee's command reached Hood's Mill around the same time as Stuart reached Cooksville. Arriving just after dawn on June 29, Lee's cavalrymen occupied the B&O Railroad, tore up track, and cut the telegraph lines severing one of the Army of the Potomac's last means of communication with Washington, D.C.

Stuart's men continued their destruction of track and telegraph lines in Sykesville. "The bridge at Sykesville was burned, and the track tore up at Hood's Mills," wrote Stuart. "Measures were taken to intercept trains . . .various telegraph lines were likewise cut, and communications of the enemy with Washington City thus cut off at every point." Confederate cavalry occupied the railroad with

The Civil War Trails marker and Maryland Civil War Centennial marker in Cooksville, Maryland. Near here, elements of Stuart's column skirmished with a Federal detachment heading towards a defensive position along the B&O Railroad. (dw)

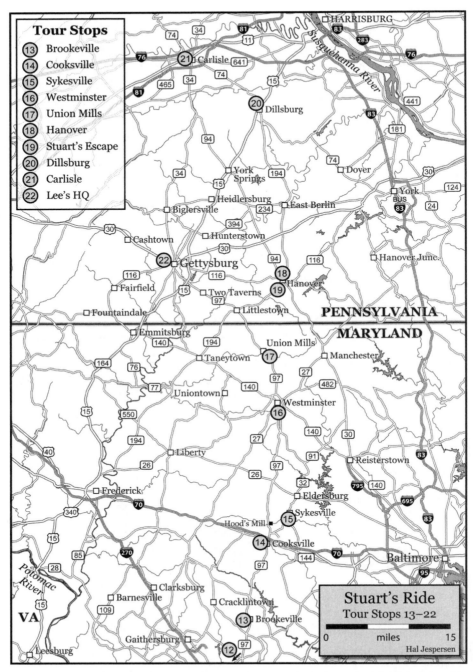

STUART'S RIDE—As Stuart sought to replicate one of his notable circles around the Union army, his ride took him farther and farther away from Lee's infantry. Ordered to connect with Ewell's infantry, Stuart's cavalry operated alone in central Maryland and Pennsylvania. By the time he sought to reconnect with Ewell, the battle of Gettysburg was already beginning.

continued operations in this area. Stuart learned here that the Army of the Potomac had a new commanding officer. Since Hooker had been relieved from command a day before, rumor spread that a special train may be taking him to Washington through Stuart's vicinity that morning. Confederate troopers tore up track in hopes of capturing the former commanding general. An alert railroad engineer, however, noticed the Confederate efforts, reversed his train to Frederick, and warned Hooker. By the end of the day, Stuart's men moved on to Westminster, Maryland, but so had Union cavalry.

A modern view of the main street in Sykesville, Maryland. Stuart's command hatched a plan from here to capture the recently relieved Joe Hooker. (dw)

Remain on Route 851 north through Sykesville for 1 mile (the road will make a sharp right turn in town). Turn left onto Route 32 (Sykesville Road) and travel 1 mile, then make a left onto Freedom Avenue. After 0.9 miles, make a right onto Johnsville Road, travel 0.3 miles and make a left onto Route 26 (Liberty Road). Travel Route 26 for 2.9 miles and take the right exit for Route 97 north (New Washington Road). Remain on Route 97 (New Washington Road) for 8.1 miles and take a left onto Hook Road. In 0.3 miles, take a right onto Washington Road and travel 0.7 miles to make a left onto South Center Street. After 0.5 miles, take a left into the entrance of the Carroll County Farm Museum. The Civil War Trails sign is to the left of the entrance.

GPS: N 39° .560262 W 76° .992957

STOP 16: WESTMINSTER

Stuart received intelligence that the Union army was concentrated around Frederick and, according to his campaign report, "it was important for me to reach our column . . . to acquaint the commanding general with the nature of the enemy's movements, as well as to place with his column my cavalry force." In order to achieve this, Stuart's troopers pushed on until they reached Westminster at nearly 5:00 p.m. Long rides were becoming commonplace for the men. Riding from Brookeville, they had a twenty-five mile ride to reach Westminster, while those who left from Hood's Mill had seventeen miles. "At this place, our advance was obstinately disputed," Stuart wrote, referring to elements of the 1st Delaware Cavalry under Maj. N. B. Knight, who engaged advance elements of the Confederate cavalry column at Westminster. A sharp but brisk fight took place down Main Street, and Union forces

This modern photograph shows the site of Corbit's Charge, in Westminster, Maryland. Although the fighting was brief, soldiers returned to Westminster after the battle of Gettysburg to recover from wounds and await transport to larger, more permanent hospitals. (dw)

eventually scattered. Most of the 85 Delaware horse soldiers, including their commander, Capt. Charles Corbit, were captured during this ill-advised charge, and two Virginia lieutenants were killed. Stuart and his men took pride in the "[s]everal flags and one piece of artillery" that were captured during and after the fight. With the brief encounter over, Stuart sent out foraging parties, and finding an abundance of supplies in the area, the men had—for the first time in a week—enough to eat. With stomachs full and mounts rested, the head of the cavalry column, Lee's brigade, reached Union Mills, Maryland, half way between Littlestown, Pennsylvania, and Westminster, Maryland. During the night of June 29 Stuart's column was stretched out between the two points, camping for the evening.

From the Carroll County Farm Museum, make a left onto South Center Street and travel 0.9 miles. Make a right onto East Main Street. In 500 feet, there are two Civil War Trails signs on the right side of the street. These markers are a continuation of the first Westminster related marker you saw.

GPS: N 39° .569764 W 76° .990501

There are also interpretive markers in front of the county courthouse focusing on the Gettysburg campaign and the fighting at Westminster. The courthouse is located at the corner of North Court Street and Court Lane.

GPS: N 39° .570914 W 76° .989067

After reading the Civil War Trails signs, turn around and head northwest on East Main Street. Continue on East Main Street and take a slight right on Pennsylvania Avenue. Remain on Pennsylvania Avenue (which will turn into Route 97 north – Littlestown Pike) for 6.5 miles and make a right into the Union Mills Homestead Park. In a few hundred feet, three Civil War Trails signs are on your right. The parking lot is straight ahead. Please be sure to visit the historic Union Mills Homestead.

GPS: N 39° .666953 W 77° .017541

STOP 17: UNION MILLS

The head of Stuart's column, Fitz Lee's brigade, arrived at Union Mills, Maryland, before nightfall on June 29. The properties at this crossroads were owned by Andrew and William Shriver—brothers and families divided by the war. Lee's brigade stretched out for the evening in the Shrivers's tannery, gristmill, sawmill, yard, and orchard. Lee himself bedded down under an apple tree in the orchard behind the Shriver home. The rest of Lee's and Stuart's columns camped on the Littlestown Turnpike, which ran through Union Mills and back to Westminster.

Stuart arrived before daybreak on June 30 and gathered his commanding officers to discuss the next move and the threat of Union cavalry operating in Littlestown and Hanover, Pennsylvania. Once at the property, William Shriver, who supported the Confederacy, invited the officers and their staffs to breakfast with his family. His daughter Sally later recorded, "Our table [was] surrounded by so many shining lights—Majors, Colonels, Captains, Doctors, and to crown all, those two noble Generals (Fitzhugh) Lee and Stuart who sang 'If you want to be a bully boy, join the cavalry'." Stuart decided to move to Hanover. The columns soon left the Shrivers, heading towards Pennsylvania.

The Shriver family homestead, including one of the mills pictured here, was owned by the family for six generations. The Shrivers hosted a meal for Confederate officers before daybreak on June 30. Today, the homestead is operated by the Union Mills Homestead Foundation. (dw)

Return to Route 97 (Littlestown Pike) and make a right; travel 0.2 miles and take a right onto Old Hanover Road. Stay on Old Hanover Road for 4.3 miles (you will cross the Mason-Dixon line at the 3.8 mile mark). Turn right onto Old Westminster Road and travel 4.9 miles (Old Westminster Road will become Westminster Road). Take a right onto Route 194 (Frederick Street) and travel 0.7 miles to the city square. Find street parking near the square. There are several Civil War markers around the square, as well as the Picket Monument, honoring all the Federal cavalry that fought at Hanover. We encourage you to take the walking tour of Civil War sites in Hanover. Visit www.civilwartraveler.com/EAST/PA/Hanover.html for a list of the markers.

GPS: N 39° .800181 W 76° .983407

STOP 18: HANOVER

Union General Kilpatrick's division spent the predawn hours of June 30 in Littlestown taking care of his men and mounts. Nearing dawn, this column of cavalry made its way toward Hanover. Beyond was

A June-July 1863 image of Hanover Junction, Pennsylvania, where yet another cavalry engagement erupted between Stuart's cavalry and Federal troopers. (loc)

their objective: York, Pennsylvania. As the lead elements of the division approached Hanover, they collided with Chambliss's brigade. Chambliss's lead regiment "not only repulsed the enemy, but drove him pell-mell through the town with half his numbers, capturing his ambulances, and a large number of prisoners. . . ." But the Confederate cavalry was only initially successful.

Take Frederick Street south from the Hanover Square for 0.7 miles and take a left onto Westminster Avenue. In 0.2 miles you will come to a bridge that crosses a small ditch. During the war, this ditch was nearly 15 feet wide and deeper than it is today. On the left side of the street is where Jeb Stuart crossed the ditch to escape Federal cavalry.

GPS: N 39° .790231 W 76° .990120

STOP 19: HANOVER: STUART'S ESCAPE

Additional Union reinforcements soon arrived on the scene, counterattacked, and began the process of throwing up barricades in the streets. The Federal reinforcements, with Brig. Gen. Farnsworth at their head, sent the Confederate cavalry rearward in confusion. Hand-to-hand fighting between opponents, and the chaos that ensued, led to the near capture of Stuart. A number of Federal troopers chased and attacked Stuart's headquarters staff during the fight. Stuart made his escape with a leap of faith in his horse Virginia hurtling across a wide, water-filled ditch.

The defensive works the Union reinforcements had built acted as a force multiplier as they awaited more support. After a short break in the skirmish, Michigan troopers under the command of George Custer arrived. Custer's men fought dismounted in a pitched back-and-forth action with Confederate cavalry. Confederate reinforcements, slow to arrive, finally bolstered the Southern line. "After a fight of about two hours, in which the whole command at different times was engaged, I made a vigorous attack upon their center, forced them back . . . and finally succeeded in breaking [their] center," Kilpatrick reported to Pleasonton that evening. Only darkness

Modern view of the ditch that Stuart's mount had to jump in order to escape capture. (cm)

brought an end to the fight, and with it, the retreat of the Confederate cavalry from the field.

Turn around, return to Frederick Street, and make a right. Travel 0.7 miles to the Hanover Square and take a left onto Carlisle Street (Route 94 north). Remain on Route 94 north for 15.4 miles and take a right onto Route 15 north. Travel 8.3 miles and make a right onto West Harrisburg Street. In 0.3 miles, take a left onto North Baltimore Street. Travel 0.3 miles and the historic Dills Tavern will be on your left. A county historic marker concerning Dillsburg's role during Stuart's ride to Gettysburg is on your right.

GPS: N 40° .115336 W 77° .036759

STOP 20: DILLSBURG

Following the engagement at Hanover, Stuart's column continued to move in an arc northward and to the west. By now, July 1, time was of the essence, and Stuart knew he needed to find Ewell's infantry, which he presumed was in the Carlisle area. "I still believed that most of our army was before Harrisburg, and justly regarded a march to Carlisle as the most likely to place me in communication with the main army," Stuart wrote. His horses and his men were near worn out from the constant moving with little sleep. Their rations were also nearly exhausted, and the Confederates entered Dillsburg near noon on July 1. The men reportedly robbed the local stores and even the post office. Just north of Dillsburg, Stuart left behind 125 wagons so the column could speed up its pace. Brigadier General Wade Hampton and his brigade remained behind at Dillsburg as Stuart moved to Carlisle. Meanwhile, unknown to Stuart or his men, the battle of Gettysburg was well under way.

Continue north on Baltimore Street and take a right onto Route 15 north. Once on Route 15 north, take your first left onto Route 74 (York Road). Stay on Route 74 for 9.1 miles. There will be a historic marker on the right at the intersection of York Road and Valley Street. In this vicinity, the Confederate cavalry and artillery arrived before Carlisle on the afternoon of July 1. Continue 0.8 miles and take a left onto East High Street. At the intersection was the location of the Carlisle Gas Works that Stuart burned. The main Confederate line was directly to your right. After you make the turn onto East High Street, travel 0.6 miles, and the Civil War Trails markers will be on your right next to the Cumberland Valley Visitors Center and the Cumberland Historical Society. If you

The Picket Monument, located in the center of Hanover, commemorates the Federal cavalry that participated in the battle at Hanover. (dw)

The Cumberland County Court House still bears the marks of Confederate shelling, such as the shell damage partway up the center column. (mw)

Brig. Gen. William "Baldy" Smith was a West Point graduate, instructor of mathematics, and career army officer in the prewar army. Although he rose to the rank of major general and commanded a corps in the Army of the Potomac, the fallout from the Union defeat at Fredericksburg relegated him to command of militia in the Department of the Susquehanna with the rank of brigadier general during the Gettysburg campaign. (loc)

have time, visit Dickenson College and the U.S. Army Heritage Museum. Carlisle Barracks is still an active military base.

GPS: N 40° .201738 W 77° .191006

STOP 21: CARLISLE

Stuart fully expected to find Confederate infantry in the area of Carlisle and believed that he would reconnect with the main army, resupply his men, and give them much-needed rest. But as Stuart arrived on the eastern outskirts of Carlisle, he found not Confederate infantry but Federal forces numbering 2,600 under Brig. Gen. William "Baldy" Smith. Smith had arrived in Carlisle earlier on July 1 with his inexperienced force of militia and cavalry. Several Confederate columns had already moved through during the previous days, and Carlisle survived mostly unscathed. Even the Carlisle Barracks military post was not harmed, but now with Stuart approaching from the east, Smith determined to fight.

Stuart, worried that he might be facing portions of the Army of the Potomac with worn-out men, decided to be cautious. He sent a flag of truce into town demanding its surrender. Smith refused. Stuart then ordered his artillery to bombard the town. He also ordered the gas works and the buildings of the Carlisle Barracks burned. Smith's men, heavily outnumbered, made no attempt to attack the Confederates. Word soon reached Stuart that a large battle had taken place south of Carlisle in the town of Gettysburg. Receiving direct orders from Lee to report to Gettysburg, Stuart began to move his cavalry south in the early morning of July 2.

After hours on the march Stuart announced near sunup that he would halt and sleep for two hours. His staff did the same. Two hours later, Stuart arose and headed toward Gettysburg. He left many in his personal column behind, asleep.

To reach Gettysburg, take High Street to Route 34 south (South Hanover Street). Travel south for 7 miles and turn left to remain on Route 34 (Yates Street/Carlisle Road). Continue south on Route 34 (Carlisle Road/Biglerville Road) for 20 miles to the Gettysburg Square and take a right onto Route 30 west (Chambersburg Street).

In 0.3 miles, take a right onto Route 30 west (Buford Avenue). In 0.5 miles, Lee's Headquarters is on the right.

GPS: N 39° .834864 W 77° .245150

STOP 22: LEE'S HEADQUARTERS

Stuart arrived in Gettysburg between noon and 1:00 p.m. on Thursday, July 2, 1863. What happened next has been written and rewritten numerous times by those who were there and those who were not. When Stuart rode up to Lee, the commander reportedly said, "Well, General Stuart, you are here at last." No record exists of the rest of their conversation. However, H.B. McClellan wrote years later that the conversation "was painful beyond description."

The widow Mary Thomson's home along the Chambersburg Pike west of Gettysburg served as General Lee's headquarters during the battle. In 2015, the Civil War Trust purchased the building and surrounding property, with plans to turn it over to the National Park Service and restore the landscape. (loc)

Stuart was finally reunited with the army. He was ordered to move to the Confederate left. Throughout the remainder of the afternoon, Fitz Lee's and Chambliss's commands, with their horse artillery, arrived on the Confederate left. Southern circles soon thereafter began debating the impact of "Stuart's Ride" on the outcome of the Pennsylvania campaign, a debate that continues today among historians.

This concludes the "Jeb Stuart's Ride" tour route. To obtain a tour brochure to the Gettysburg battlefield, visit the Gettysburg National Military Park Visitor Center at 1195 Baltimore Pike, Gettysburg, Pennsylvania 17325. If you are interested, the "Retreat from Gettysburg" chapter begins at the nearby Seminary Ridge Museum, located at 111 Seminary Ridge, Gettysburg, Pennsylvania 17325.

The Battle

CHAPTER FOUR

Hours after the first shot of the battle of Gettysburg was fired on July 1, 1863, Buford's troopers were under increasing pressure fighting dismounted on the ridges west of Gettysburg. Sending a message to Army headquarters, Buford wrote, "The enemy's force (A.P. Hill's) are advancing on me at this point, and driving my pickets and skirmishers very rapidly. There is also a large force at Heidlersburg that is driving my pickets at that point from that direction. General Reynolds is advancing, and is within 3 miles of this point with his leading division. I am positive that the whole of A.P. Hill's force is advancing."

Help was on the way. Brigadier General James Wadsworth, a divisional commander in I Corps, recalled his corps's arrival to the battlefield: "He [Reynolds] immediately turned the head of the column to the left, across the fields, and struck the Cashtown road about three-quarters of a mile west of Gettysburg at about 10 a.m. Here we met the advance guard of the enemy." It was a severe fight, boiling through such places as Herbst Woods and an unfinished railroad cut. It was not long until both forces on the field were thoroughly drained of energy and men—among them Gen. Reynolds, killed shortly after arriving on the scene.

The High Water Mark monument stands near the copse of trees, marking the point of farthest advance for the Confederate army during their climactic attack on the third day of the battle. (cm)

Not long after a lull settled on the farm fields west of town, Confederate reinforcements from the Second Corps, Ewell's, arrived on Oak Hill. The troops, from Gen. Rodes's division, arrived at just the right time

Brig. Gen. James Wadsworth, a division commander in Gen. Reynolds's I Corps, had some of the first Federal infantry engaged in the battle of Gettysburg on July 1, 1863. (loc)

and place. "On arriving on the field," Rodes recalled, "I found that by keeping along the wooded ridge, on the left side of which the town of Gettysburg is situated, I could strike the force of the enemy with which Gen. Hill's troops were engaged upon the flank, and that, besides moving under cover, whenever we struck the enemy we could engage him with the advantage of ground." Soon after his arrival, Rodes ordered his brigades forward against Union reinforcements on Oak Ridge. The attacks were disjointed and piecemeal and repulsed each time with significant loss. Still, Rodes's arrival blocked an extension of the Federal line.

As Rodes's division pushed forward its attack from Oak Hill, more Confederate units arrived due north of Gettysburg. General Early's division took a position in a west-to-east line of battle with their right flank attempting in vain to connect with Rodes's left. Opposite Early's position were Union soldiers from the XI Corps. These men had pushed on to Gettysburg in a hard march through the early morning hours. One of the XI Corps's division commanders, Brig. Gen. Francis Barlow, did not like the flat, open ground which his men were ordered to occupy. A half mile to his front was an exposed knoll—high ground—that he believed was a far better defensive position than the one he occupied. Without orders from his superiors, Barlow ordered his men to move out and take a defensive stance on the knoll.

Within moments of Barlow's arrival, Early's Confederate artillery shelled the position: "[A] fire was opened upon the enemy's infantry and artillery by my artillery with considerable effect." With the barrage underway, Early's brigades moved toward the advanced and exposed position. Union defenders of the knoll fell victim to the Confederate onslaught. One of Early's

A view of the Railroad Cut taken by Mumper and Co. between 1866-1889. (loc)

Robert Rodes described a "wooded-ridge"— Oak Hill—in his report of the battle. (dw)

brigades, Gen. Gordon's, assailed the knoll from the north, while a brigade from Rodes's division, Brig. Gen. George Doles's, attacked the exposed Federal position from the west. "After a short but hot contest, Gordon succeeded in routing the force opposed to him," Early later wrote, "and drove it back with great slaughter, capturing, among a number of prisoners, General Barlow himself, who was severely wounded."

Herbst Woods, also known as Reynold's Woods, was the scene of heavy fighting during the battle of July 1 and the site of the mortal wounding of Gen. Reynolds. (loc)

With the collapse of Barlow's advanced position and the retreat of other units along the length of the Federal line, it was not long before a full retreat of the entire position occurred. From his vantage point on Oak Hill, Rodes witnessed the victory and later recorded, "The enemy was thus routed at all points." The remnants of the I and XI Corps groped their way through town as they retreated towards a rallying point south of Gettysburg: Cemetery Hill. This dominating piece of terrain commanded the town itself and several critical roads to Gettysburg from the south and southeast, such as the Emmitsburg Road, Taneytown Road, and Baltimore

LEFT: Prewar lawyer Brig. Gen. Francis Barlow enlisted at the outbreak of the war as a private in a militia regiment. By June 1863, he commanded a division in the derided XI Corps of the Army of the Potomac. His forward movement of his troops on the afternoon of July 1 north of Gettysburg remains a controversy in Gettysburg historiography to this day. (loc)

RIGHT: A native Georgian and prewar businessman, Brig. Gen. George Doles and his brigade of Georgians attacked fiercely on July 1, helping push the advanced XI Corps line rearward towards Gettysburg. (loc)

Pike. General Oliver Otis Howard had secured Cemetery Hill earlier during the day and now the position was put into service.

While the Union army at Gettysburg was in full retreat, Maj. Gen. Winfield Scott Hancock arrived in Gettysburg at the order of General Meade to take command on the field. Howard and Hancock, despite tensions over the order, worked to build a strong defensive position on Cemetery Hill, not knowing if the Confederate army would continue its attack. Although Gen. Lee ordered a continued push, particularly by the Second Corps, further Confederate attacks did not come against the reorganized Union position.

Throughout the evening of July 1 and into July 2, more reinforcements for both armies continued to march toward the scene of the day's fighting. One of the most important arrivals for the Army of the Potomac was Meade himself, who quickly established his headquarters in the home of Lydia Leister along the Taneytown Road at the southern foot of Cemetery Hill. Gathering his staff, Meade rode along the position the army had taken before his arrival and sketched out a line of battle for the remainder of the corps for when they, too, arrived. In all, the Army of the Potomac's line of battle south of Gettysburg ran roughly three miles from Culp's Hill on the right, northwest to Cemetery Hill, and then south towards the Round Tops along a ridge extending from Cemetery Hill itself.

As Meade worked to secure his army in the best

possible position early during the morning of July 2,
Robert E. Lee summoned to his headquarters, west of
Gettysburg, a young captain named Samuel Johnston.
Lee planned to renew the attack for the second day
but needed vital information as to where the left flank
of the Federal army rested. Lee's plan called for a
strong assault on the left of the Union line, hopefully
rolling it up in the process. Johnston left headquarters
around 4:00 a.m. and returned roughly three hours
later. Although he could not say exactly where the
Federal left flank ended, he told Lee that no Union
soldiers were present on and in the vicinity of the
Round Tops where his reconnaissance had taken him.
The Army of Northern Virginia went to work making
the necessary preparations for the day ahead with, at
best, sketchy intelligence.

As the morning wore on, along the Union lines,
Meade faced his first challenge of the day. The Union
army fought on the defensive July 1, and now he
looked to go on the offensive. The army commander
wanted to launch an assault from his right but
scouting and intelligence convinced him otherwise.
Meade's second challenge of the day came on his left,
from New York politician and III Corps commander
Maj. Gen. Daniel Sickles. Meade had placed the III
Corps on the army's left flank, but Sickles perceived
numerous problems with the position and issued
orders to his corps to advance to a new position.
Captain George E. Randolph, the III Corps's chief of
artillery, recalled three months later, "Between 1 and
2 p.m. Major-General Sickles notified me that he was
about to change his line, throwing his right forward
to the high ground, running his line from Round Top

A view of Culp's Hill from
East Cemetery Hill. This
position served as the right
flank of the Army of the
Potomac's battleline. (loc)

A view of Little Round Top, left, and Big Round Top, right. The Round Tops comprised the left flank of the Army of the Potomac's battleline. (loc)

Maj. Gen. Daniel Sickles was the only corps commander in the Army of the Potomac during the Gettysburg campaign with no formal military training. A political appointment with strong ties and support, Sickles told a skewed version of events at Gettysburg on July 2. His version has impacted the battle's history for more than 150 years. (loc)

Mountain, on the left, to a peach orchard on the Emmitsburg road, and thence along the road toward Gettysburg to a second orchard." When Meade heard of the movement, he rode to his left and met with Sickles near the now-famous Peach Orchard. "General Sickles this is neutral ground," Meade said. "Our guns command it, as well as the enemy's, the very reason you cannot hold applies to them." Meade promised reinforcements and rode back for headquarters. The III Corps line would remain where it was. It was nearing 4:00 p.m., and the Confederates were preparing their attack.

Lee selected Longstreet's Corps to lead the assault. Longstreet's far-right units, anchoring the right of the Rebel army, were the first to make contact with the new line of the Army of the Potomac. Fighting swirled around places like Little Round Top, Devil's Den, and the Triangular Field. As the attack continued, the fighting spread northward. New struggles opened at the Wheatfield, Stony Hill, the Peach Orchard and along the Emmitsburg Road. As the sun neared the horizon, more Confederate units from Florida, Georgia, and other southern states entered the fray and pushed hard toward Cemetery Ridge. The setting sun and a lack of more units committed to the attack ended the fighting in this sector of the Federal line. However, the day's battle was far from over.

Lee's plan of attack for July 2 was twofold. The main Confederate attack fell to Longstreet and came from the Confederate right, hoping to roll up the left flank of the Union army. When Longstreet's assault got underway, the Second Corps under Richard Ewell was supposed to launch a feint against the Federal right, along Culp's Hill and Cemetery Hill. If Ewell thought it was wise, then he should launch an assault on the Federal position. Lee's strategy, in adding this assault, was to pin these Federal soldiers of the I, XI, and XII Corps to the Federal right, leaving them unable to assist their comrades-in-arms on the other end of the line. Nearing 5:00 p.m. on July 2,

An unidentified photographer took this image, "Scene of the charge of the Louisiana Tigers... taken from Cemetery Hill at about position of right gun of Wiedrich's Battery," in July 1863. (loc)

Second Corps artillery on Benner's Hill unleashed a furious barrage against Union artillery on Cemetery Hill. Federal artillery quickly replied. The contest was one-sided, and after nearly ninety minutes of sustained bombardment at a distance of 1,400 yards, the Rebel artillery was forced off the hill. By 7:30 p.m., the Confederate infantry had already engaged a lone Union brigade on Culp's Hill. Lee's plan failed on this front, after the Union left flank was strengthened by the delayed arrival of the XII Corps. Now Confederate soldiers from Louisiana and North Carolina moved forward to join in the attack. They broke through the Union defenses at the base of the eastern approach to Cemetery Hill, but as darkness consumed the battlefield, only a few Confederates reached the summit. Despite their low numbers, they fought desperately in hand-to-hand combat, silenced the Federal batteries atop the hill, and occupied the position. Within fifteen minutes, however, reinforcements from the II and XI Corps

A painting by Edwin Forbes depicting a "Scene behind the breastworks on Culps Hill, morning of July 3rd 1863." (loc)

LEFT: Maj. Gen. Isaac Trimble returned to the Army of Northern Virginia during the later phases of the Gettysburg campaign without a command. Trimble had been recovering from a grievous wound received at the battle of Second Manassas in August of 1862 when Gen. Lee started northward in June 1863. Trimble was again wounded during the Confederate attack on the afternoon of July 3. (loc)

RIGHT: Maj. Gen. George Pickett, a West Point graduate and veteran of the Mexican and Pig Wars, saw his first combat during the Civil War during the Peninsula campaign in 1862. Pickett's command and its role during the Confederate attack on July 3 simultaneously increased Pickett's fame while at the same time marked a command tragedy. (loc)

arrived on the field and sent the Confederate infantry back down Cemetery Hill. The breach was sealed.

The fighting on July 2 finally came to an end. Meade called his corps commanders and other ranking staff to a council of war at his headquarters along the Taneytown Road. At the end of the meeting, three decisions were made regarding the strategy for the Union army during the coming days. First, the Union army would remain at Gettysburg. Second, they would remain on the defensive. Lastly, if the Confederates did not attack the Federal position within the next forty-eight hours, the Union army would go on the offensive.

Meanwhile, at Lee's headquarters along the Chambersburg Pike, "the general plan was unchanged," Lee later wrote. The main Confederate attack would once again come from the right. Meanwhile, the Second Corps would renew their assaults from the Confederate left.

By 4:00 a.m., July 3, 1863, light skirmishing began as the XII Corps returned to Culp's Hill from the Federal left flank. Within thirty minutes, the fighting in this area escalated into some of the hardest attacks and defenses of the entire battle. As the fighting in this sector raged, the startling lack of a Confederate attack on their right presented a problem for Lee.

The   General's   "unchanged"

The fields of Pickett's Charge taken during the postwar era from Cemetery Ridge. (gnmp)

plan entailed a coordinated attack on both flanks of the Federal position simultaneously. Lee's orders left a lot of latitude for his generals, and his orders for this attack was no different. Although it specified the attack to take place the "next morning," no exact time was given. This latitude allowed General Longstreet to seek other alternatives to the "unchanged" plan. When Lee arrived to the Confederate right and met with Longstreet on the morning of July 3, Lee's confidence in a final victory at Gettysburg that morning deflated as Longstreet's "dispositions were not completed as early as was expected." Longstreet's time investment in other alternatives left his corps unready to attack simultaneously with the Second Corps. Ewell's men could not continue at the pace at which the fight for Culp's Hill had reached. The Second Corps was quickly expending men, energy, and ammunition with each subsequent assault on the well-defended position. There would not be time for Longstreet's assault on the Confederate right to get off the ground. The uncoordinated attack between the two corps forced Lee to create a new plan for the remainder of July 3.

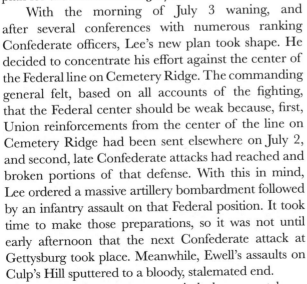

"Pickett's charge from a position on the enemy's line looking toward the Union lines, Ziegler's grove on the left, clump of trees on right" by Edwin Forbes. (loc)

With the morning of July 3 waning, and after several conferences with numerous ranking Confederate officers, Lee's new plan took shape. He decided to concentrate his effort against the center of the Federal line on Cemetery Ridge. The commanding general felt, based on all accounts of the fighting, that the Federal center should be weak because, first, Union reinforcements from the center of the line on Cemetery Ridge had been sent elsewhere on July 2, and second, late Confederate attacks had reached and broken portions of that defense. With this in mind, Lee ordered a massive artillery bombardment followed by an infantry assault on that Federal position. It took time to make those preparations, so it was not until early afternoon that the next Confederate attack at Gettysburg took place. Meanwhile, Ewell's assaults on Culp's Hill sputtered to a bloody, stalemated end.

"At ten minutes to one precisely, by my watch . . .

Brig. Gen. Lewis Armistead received two wounds once he and his men crossed the stone wall. He was later evacuated to the XI Corps field hospital at the George Spangler farm where he died on the morning of July 5, 1863. (lova)

a heavy gun was heard from the enemy's line," wrote Thomas F. Galwey of the 8th Ohio Volunteer Infantry. "Instinct told us at once that that gun had fired a signal." It was indeed a signal, fired by Confederate artillery near the Peach Orchard on the right of the Confederate line. Soon, approximately 150 other Confederate guns zeroed in on Cemetery Ridge. Destruction along the ridge mounted quickly. After nearly two hours of sustained firing, the Confederate artillery slackened their fire to only sporadic shots along the ridge. Many Confederate batteries' ammunition chests were low or empty, and those monitoring the effect of the cannonade felt that they accomplished all they could. It was time for the Confederate infantry to move forward.

At 3:00 p.m., the Confederate infantry from three divisions of two different corps began the earliest movements of the assault. Those units were selected from a fresh division of Virginians commanded by George Pickett, First Corps, and two divisions from the Third Corps, both with new divisional commanders, James J. Pettigrew and Isaac Trimble. Nearly 12,000 Rebel soldiers advanced across an open field around numerous obstacles—fence lines, orchards, undulating terrain, and numerous farm buildings—all while under fire from long-range Union artillery. As the attacking infantry reached the Emmitsburg Road, the Rebel infantry ran into their biggest obstacles yet. The road was lined on both sides with a strong post-and-rail fence. Only a few portions had been taken down over the previous two days. Confederate

A modern image of where Brig. Gen. Lewis Armistead and 100-150 Confederate soldiers broke through the Union defenses on Cemetery Ridge. (dw)

infantry was forced to go up and over long portions of two fence lines, slowing the momentum of the attack considerably and decimating unit cohesion, command, and control.

Assisting in confounding the Confederate attack, Federal cannon now switched to close-range, anti-personnel canister fire, sending unimaginable amounts of lead into the air. In addition, having held their fire, Union infantry opened up for the first time. Casualties in the attacking column mounted in staggering numbers. Still, the dwindling numbers pushed on. Regiments were only so in name. Pockets of Confederate soldiers slowed their advance to a crawl and, for the first time, returned fire. The left flank of the assaulting force had long since given way and the right was under a severe flank attack. Between 100 and 150 Confederate soldiers broke the Union line along a right angle of a stonewall on Cemetery Ridge. Moments later, the officer who led those men over the wall, Brig. Gen. Lewis Armistead, was on the ground with two wounds. Union reinforcements rushed to the area of the breakthrough from all directions. Confederate soldiers who did not surrender, or had been wounded or killed, retreated back to Seminary Ridge.

The charge, the Pickett-Pettigrew-Trimble Assault, was over and so was the engagement at Gettysburg. Lee had committed the remaining elements of his army to this attack, and now his casualties and ammunition levels dictated a retreat. After sending orders to prepare to defend against an attack from Meade, Lee worked to make plans to extricate his army from Pennsylvania—and quickly.

The Retreat From Gettysburg

CHAPTER FIVE

On July 4, a terrible deluge of rain marked the anniversary of the country's founding. The rains proved to be a challenge for both armies as they prepared for their next moves.

Despite nature's wrath, the men of the Union army had much reason to celebrate this Fourth of July. In response to the army's victory, Meade prepared General Orders No. 68 congratulating his men. "The commanding general, in behalf of the country, thanks the Army of the Potomac for the glorious result of the recent operations," wrote Meade. He also made it known to the army that they could not rest because the campaign was not over. "Our task is not yet accomplished, and the commanding general looks to the army for greater efforts to drive from our soil every vestige of the presence of the invader."

Meade's selection of words, much to the chagrin of President Lincoln, laid out a strategy not for the destruction of the Confederate army, but for relieving Pennsylvania of the Confederate presence. Meade's subordinates shared their commander's mindset, though. Nearly all his corps commanders voted against going on the offensive during a second council of war Meade had held on July 4. Instead, the Army of the Potomac would utilize its cavalry for the time being. The stage was now set for next phase of the Gettysburg campaign.

Lee knew the Army of Northern Virginia's time

A modern image, this view from High Rock overlooks Cumberland Valley, site of several cavalry engagements during the Confederate retreat. (dw)

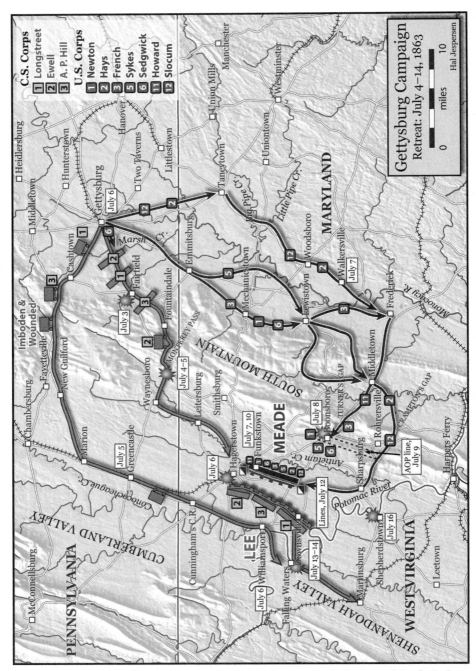

RETREAT FROM GETTYSBURG: JULY 4-14, 1863—Perhaps the least studied aspect of the Gettysburg campaign the retreat of the Confederate army demonstrated superb handling of wagon and ambulance train evacuation while the pursuit by the Army of the Potomac left much to be desired.

in Pennsylvania was limited. During the evening of July 3, 1863, he and other top-ranking Confederate officers had met to determine the order and route of retreat out of the state. Based on maps and intelligence, Lee determined that the army would use a series of roads that led from Gettysburg, over South Mountain at Monterey Pass, to Williamsport, Maryland, and across the Potomac River to the safety of Virginia. Consequently, Lee ordered Brig. Gen. John Imboden to headquarters. During his meeting with the cavalryman, Lee not only laid out the army's next move but also the enormous task ahead for Imboden's command. "We must now return to Virginia," Lee sadly intoned. "As many of our poor wounded as possible must be taken home. I have sent for you, because your men and horses are fresh and in good condition, to guard and conduct our train back to Virginia. The duty will be arduous, responsible, and dangerous, for I am afraid you will be harassed by the enemy's cavalry." After covering details of the planned route of retreat, the meeting between Lee and Imboden broke up around 2:00 a.m. The Confederate withdrawal from Pennsylvania was about to begin.

Imboden had a massive endeavor before him. His 2,100 Virginia cavalrymen and six field pieces were tasked with the escort of hundreds of slow-moving wagons filled beyond capacity with thousands of wounded men. Imboden quickly realized his tall task would take time and not be one of expedience. The general hoped to leave early on the morning of July 4, but it took far longer to assemble the train of wagons, ambulances, and the walking wounded.

That afternoon, several different Union commands sent out probes to ascertain the extent of the new Confederate line. By nightfall, however, that line changed as large bodies of Confederate soldiers pulled out and headed down the Fairfield Road towards designated crossing points at Williamsport and Falling Waters, Maryland. Union signalmen spotted a number of Confederate wagon trains, cattle, and soldiers leaving the area and passed the intelligence on to Meade. Falling back on his plan to utilize the Federal cavalry, Meade relied on Pleasonton to order his forces against the rear of

Lee's trains. Kilpatrick's division, along with Col. Pennock Huey's brigade, were ordered to a mountain gap south of Fairfield, Monterey Pass. Battle raged there during the late hours of July 4 and into July 5.

By 4:00 p.m. on July 4, with the 18th Virginia Cavalry and a section of the Staunton Artillery at its head, the column moved out. The sight stretched along the Chambersburg Pike from Gettysburg west towards Cashtown and Chambersburg for seventeen miles. Imboden kept the train moving throughout the rest of July 4 and until daybreak of July 5. "During this one night I realized more of the horrors of war than I had in all the two preceding years," Imboden recalled. Some of the wounded "were simply moaning; some were praying, and others uttering the most fearful oaths and execrations that despair and agony could wring from them. . . . No help could be rendered to any of the sufferers. No heed could be given to any of their appeals." The last wagon in Imboden's column did not leave Gettysburg until the afternoon of July 5.

Meanwhile, Lee consolidated his expansive battle line during the evening of July 3. The new position of the Army of Northern Virginia stretched from the Mummasburg Road northwest of Gettysburg to the Emmitsburg Road south of the Peach Orchard. It is from these positions that the army withdrew from the field of battle.

Back in Gettysburg, during the early morning hours of July 5, the final two Confederate corps, Longstreet's and Ewell's, pulled out of their line of

Taken after the battle, this contemporary image shows three Confederate prisoners on Seminary Ridge. The location is most likely near the intersection of modern day Seminary Ridge and Buford Ave. (loc)

battle and began their retreat. Meade, who received intelligence to that affect, ordered his VI Corps, as well as some cavalry and artillery, down the Fairfield Road in pursuit. In addition to these movements, Federal and Confederate cavalry engaged in Smithsburg, Maryland. Also on July 5, the Confederate wagon train of wounded, as well as the quartermaster stores, reached Williamsport, Maryland. Imboden and Maj. John Harman realized the river was too high to ford and, just the day before, Federal forces had destroyed a pontoon bridge that had been there. Any crossing of the Potomac would have to be done at Lemen's ferry, two wagons at a time.

Brig. Gen. John Imboden was tasked by Lee to escort the massive train of wounded back to the safety of Virginia. Although Imboden had some prewar militia experience, his vocation as a teacher and lawyer could not have prepared him for the arduous days ahead. (loc)

The following day, July 6, Confederate and Federal cavalry remained in the saddle, both forces operating in the area of Boonsboro and Hagerstown. Yet another cavalry clash took place at the latter.

Lee's army was in full retreat towards the Potomac. But Meade, who had received intelligence that Lee did not stop at South Mountain to make a defensive stand, ordered his army to Middletown and to use Turner's and Crampton's gaps to attack the Confederates before they could cross the Potomac River.

Several brigades of Federal cavalry were making just such an attack against a hastily constructed defensive position at Williamsport. Despite a cobbled-together defense, the Confederate line held.

By July 7, Lee's infantry had arrived at Hagerstown, Maryland. The retreat thus far had been grueling, and after organizing a defensive line, the Confederates rested for the next several days.

Meanwhile the Federal army prepared for a grueling march of its own. General Meade, based on all available intelligence, felt secure that Lee's invasion was over and that Washington was safe. He now planned to catch Lee and bring him to battle before he escaped back into Virginia. As the Federal infantry pushed hard to catch Lee over the ensuing days, he used the time to strengthen the previously cobbled-together defensive position at Williamsport. Here, Lee was stalled as his army awaited water levels to lower and a new pontoon bridge to be built. Thus on July 8, Lee, at Hagerstown with the three army corps, ordered Stuart to keep the Army of the

Maj. John Harman had served as a quartermaster in the Confederate army since May 1861 with "Stonewall" Jackson's command at Harpers Ferry. Now, following the Confederate defeat at Gettysburg, Harman, the chief quartermaster of the Confederate Second Corps, was responsible for getting all of the bounty captured during the campaign back to Virginia. (gnmp)

Potomac busy while the Southern army constructed the new position. Stuart and his four brigades did just that, battling Federal cavalry and later, infantry, at Boonsboro.

On July 9, 1863, the Confederate army continued to work on its defensive positions while the Federal army secured the several gaps in the South Mountain range and further concentrated at Boonsboro. By July 10, Meade knew the Confederate wagon train was stuck at Williamsport, but he was still unsure of the Rebel army's exact location due to the nature of the terrain in the area. To help him gather further intelligence, Meade again relied on the Federal cavalry. General Lee relied on his cavalry to keep the Federal eyes and ears far enough away from discovering his construction. These two forces collided at Funkstown. Nightfall brought an end to the battle, with the Confederate corps consolidating into the defensive works at Williamsport that evening.

The Confederate army continued throughout July 11 to dig in at Williamsport and, to the south, at Falling Waters, where a new pontoon bridge was completed the day before. Meade's army moved cautiously closer to the Confederate lines but no fighting occurred. On July 12, the Army of the Potomac moved into a line of battle opposite the Confederate defensive position. Meade held another council of war, which ultimately decided not to attack the strong Confederate works. Meanwhile, Lee—still waiting for the Potomac to drop further—ordered his wagons and ambulances to the pontoon bridge at Falling Waters where they could cross faster once the time came. Late the following evening, July 13, Lee ordered his columns to cross at both sites, Williamsport and Falling Waters.

By 11:00 a.m. on July 14, after hours of probes of the Confederate positions, Federal cavalry found the last significant body of Confederate troops yet to cross at Falling Waters and attacked. The Union thrust was kept at bay, and the final elements of the Army of Northern Virginia crossed back to Virginia.

The following "Retreat from Gettysburg" tour route is organized for the traveler's convenience according to geography; thus, for efficiency along the tour route, several tour stops are not in chronological order, but rather geographic order. If you would like to follow the events during this time period of the Gettysburg campaign in chronological order, travel to the tour stops in the following manner:

Stop 1: Fairfield
Stop 2: Battle of Monterey Pass
Stop 3: Leitersburg
Stop 4: Smithsburg
Stop 10: The Wagoner's Fight
Stop 5: Battle of Hagerstown
Stop 7: Battle of Boonsboro
Stop 6: Battle of Funkstown
Stop 9: Jones's Crossroads
Stop 8: Booth's Mill Bridge: Meade's Council of War
Stop 11: Battle of Falling Waters: Donnelly House
Stop 12: Williamsport

Note, if you choose to go to these stops in this order, do not follow the printed directions below.

Otherwise, to begin the "Retreat from Gettysburg" tour route, start your tour at the Seminary Ridge Museum located at 111 Seminary Ridge, Gettysburg, Pennsylvania 17325. There are interpretive markers here relating to the aftermath of the battle. The Seminary Ridge Museum also has great exhibits on the battle and especially its aftermath.

From the Seminary Ridge Museum, take Seminary Ridge south and make a right onto Route 116 (Fairfield Road). Travel 7.4 miles and the Fairfield Inn will be on your right. A Civil War Trails marker is located in front of the Inn.

GPS: N 39° .786980 W 77° .369527

STOP 1: FAIRFIELD

The town of Fairfield, twelve miles southwest of Gettysburg, was an important stop along the Fairfield Road for the Confederate army, both during the three-day battle and even more so during the retreat from Gettysburg.

On July 3, Lee's cavalry had fought to secure Fairfield. General Merritt had ordered the 6th United States Cavalry to Fairfield that day to locate and capture a rumored cache of slow-moving Confederate wagons in the area. It was not long before elements of the 6th, under the command of Maj. Samuel Starr, collided with the 7th Virginia Cavalry. The

Brig. Gen. Alfred Iverson, a Tuskegee Military Institute graduate and Mexican War veteran, resigned his commission with the U.S. Army at the beginning of the Civil War. Iverson's reputation began diminishing before his leadership and command performance of July 1. His greatly reduced brigade acted as an infantry support to Harman's retreating supply train. (loc)

Federal soldiers withdrew and informed Starr of the Confederate presence. Starr led the 6th to a ridge just outside of Fairfield proper where he dismounted his men. Starr's men repulsed a charge by the 7th before a second Confederate attack, supported by artillery and another regiment of cavalry, sent them rearward from their dismounted defensive position. The Confederate cavalry pursued the Federals but were unable to catch them. These Confederate units remained in and around Fairfield for the next several days, ensuring the security of one of the most vital roads to the Confederate retreat.

The Fairfield Road provided the Confederate army with one of the most direct routes to Williamsport, Maryland, and a crossing of the Potomac River back into Virginia. One element of the Confederate army to use this route was the army's reserve quartermaster and subsistence stores and wagons. These essential supplies garnished from the Pennsylvania countryside needed to get on the road if the Confederates wanted to save them. General Lee ordered the Second Corps's chief quartermaster, Maj. John Harman, to get this wagon train and supplies headed southwest along the Fairfield Road to the Pennsylvania-Maryland border. Harman's train started to move at 3:00 a.m. on July 4, followed by Ewell's trains, with Brig. Gen. Alfred Iverson's brigade acting as support, hooking up with the column after midnight. By 9:00 p.m., the head of the column reached Hagerstown—an impressive feat. The success of the retreat of the Confederate army continued to rest with the skill of the Confederate quartermaster department over the days to come.

Also on the move was General Stuart. Two of his brigades, Hampton's and Fitz Lee's, moved along the Chambersburg Pike at nightfall of July 4 to guard the army's right and Imboden's trains. The other brigades in Stuart's command, Robertson's and Jones's, headed towards Fairfield. Stuart himself followed Jenkins's and Chambliss's command toward Emmitsburg, Maryland, covering the army's left. Both of these columns needed the use of the vital Fairfield Road, a road leading to Maryland, and Lee's selected route of retreat for large portions of his army.

Today, several buildings that stood during the time of the cavalry fight at Fairfield and were later used as hospitals for the battle's casualties still stand, including the widow Sarah Amanda Blythe's house, which is the most likely location where the wounded Starr had his arm amputated. All these buildings witnessed large portions of the Confederate army retreating from Gettysburg. Especially notable are the Rufus C. Swope House, across from the Fairfield Inn; the Fairfield Inn itself; and St. John's Lutheran Church. Historic markers are located on these buildings identifying their roles in the July 3 cavalry fight and the retreat of the Confederate army.

If interested in visiting the Fairfield battlefield, take a left onto Route 116 (East Main Street) and travel 0.4 miles, then make a left onto Route 3011 (Carroll's Tract Road). Travel 2.4 miles and there will be a Gettysburg National Military Park Commission sign for Confederate Brig. Gen. William "Grumble" Jones's brigade. Continue another 0.2 miles and another marker for the 6th U.S. Cavalry will be on your left. Turn around at the next safe place and return to Fairfield to pick up the rest of the "Retreat from Gettysburg" tour.

From the Fairfield Inn, take a right onto Route 116 (West Main Street) and, in 1.2 miles, take a slight right onto Jacks Mountain Road. At the end of Jacks Mountain Road (2.7 miles), make a right onto Route 16 (Waynesboro Pike). Travel 4.3 miles and the Monterey Pass Battlefield Museum is on the right. There are several interpretive markers around the museum. Plans are in the works to interpret other parts of the battlefield with a trail from the museum. Parts of the battlefield are included in the park administered by Washington Township as a Franklin County Park; the Friends of Monterey Pass Battlefield, Inc., operates the museum.

GPS: N 39° .738093 W 77° .479810

STOP 2: BATTLE OF MONTEREY PASS
BY JOHN A. MILLER

Vital to the Confederate retreat from Pennsylvania were several important roads. The road that led through Monterey Pass was an established Pennsylvania highway that led directly to Williamsport, Maryland. During the mid 1700s, this was one of two wagon roads that led to the south. Studying maps of the area, the Hagerstown Road, locally known as the Fairfield Road, was the shortest

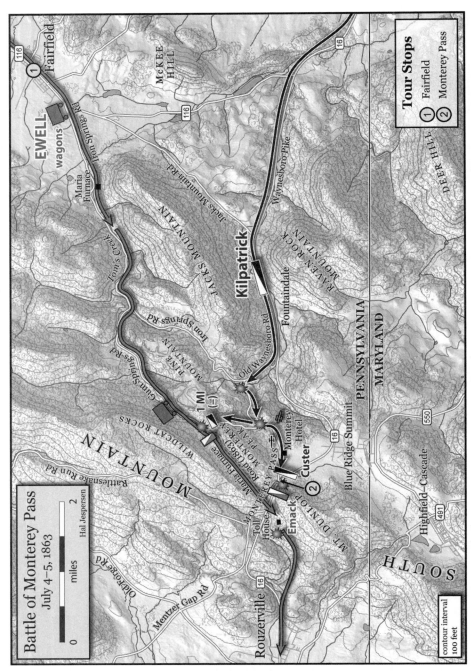

BATTLE OF MONTEREY PASS—Union and Confederate forces collided once again late in the evening of July 4 and into July 5 during a tremendous thunderstorm at Monterey Pass. Confederate forces needed to maintain this critical pass in order for one of their primary routes of retreat to the Potomac River to remain open.

An 1890 photograph of the Monterey Pass Tollhouse. (jm)

and most direct route to the safety of the Potomac River. Additionally, at Monterey Pass, several roads converged, forming a hub that was anchored by a tollgate house. No other gap in the South Mountain range had this characteristic. Whoever controlled Monterey Pass controlled the flow of traffic, so Lee desperately needed to control this area if he wished for his army to reach the safety of Virginia.

During the late afternoon of July 4, dark clouds came in from the west, and a violent thunderstorm swept through the area. The rain poured over the landscape, causing the mountain clay roads to become a muddy mess for the wagons and animals pulling them. By 9:00 p.m., with weather conditions worsening, the first Federal cavalry—on the prowl throughout much of the day—advanced to the top of the summit at the pass. As they crested the summit, a Confederate cannon fired. The battle for Monterey Pass had begun.

Instantly, about two dozen Marylanders, under Capt. George Emack, charged the Union advance. After a short skirmish, the Confederate cavalry fell back to the Monterey Inn and waited for the Union cavalry to make its next appearance. General Kilpatrick, directing the spirited affair, reorganized his forces for the next attack and selected Custer's brigade to attack up the turnpike to hit the Confederate front and right flank. He also ordered the 18th Pennsylvania Cavalry to move along Furnace Road, then head into the woods to assault the Confederate left flank.

Nearing 10:00 p.m., the Union cavalry moved again. In between lightning strikes, Emack saw these

This is the area where the old wooden bridge once spanned Red Run. Here, Col. Russell Alger charged across the bridge, filed to the left, and formed a makeshift battle line. (jm)

movements and ordered his company to fall back to Red Run where reinforcements were at hand. As Capt. William Tanner's lone cannon was withdrawing, the Pennsylvanians came out of the woods and captured the limber. Confederate cannoneers managed to save the cannon and redeployed their gun to support the cavalry at Red Run. As wagon trains with ammunition approached the Monterey tollgate house, Tanner's men resupplied their gun.

Meanwhile, Kilpatrick ordered a squadron of the 1st Michigan Cavalry, under the command of Lt. Col. Peter Stagg, to Fairfield Gap in order to block the wagons entering Monterey Pass and possibly turn the Confederate right flank. This small gap is one mile to the northeast of Monterey Pass. Using a local girl, Hetty Zeilinger, as their guide, the squadron proceeded down Furnace Road, in an additional effort to cut the wagon train in half. Shortly after midnight, Stagg came into contact with Mooreman's Battery and two companies of the 11th Virginia Cavalry, who were supported by the 5th North Carolina Cavalry. The Fairfield Gap attack was a failure, and within a few hours, the remnants of the 1st Michigan squadron fell back to the Emmitsburg and Waynesboro Turnpike. As the Michiganders left to attack Fairfield Gap, Kilpatrick ordered Lt. Col. Addison Preston's Vermont cavalry to Leitersburg, Maryland.

The rest of Custer's brigade was deployed mostly on the right of the Emmitsburg and Waynesboro Turnpike and ordered to cut the wagon train in half. As they moved through the thick woods toward Red Run, fighting became fierce. With darkness and heavy rain, soldiers had to be guided by sound and senses rather than sight. Both Union and Confederate cavalrymen who were dismounted in the woods literally had only seconds to distinguish objects in their front after a flash of lightning or small arms fire illuminated the landscape.

By 3:30 a.m., after several hours of hard fighting, Col. Russell Alger of the 5th Michigan Cavalry, supported by artillery, led a charge across the bridge spanning Red Run. He quickly deployed his men forming a makeshift battle line. The Confederate cavalry, now reinforced by additional units, also deployed at the Monterey tollgate house. Confederate reinforcements arrived from Fairfield Gap as well as from Waterloo. Needing reinforcements as well, Custer received the 1st West Virginia Cavalry and Company A of the 1st Ohio Cavalry. Orders were soon given to charge the Confederate positions, and the two reinforcing units charged across the bridge and took prisoners and wagons. Confederate cavalry deployed on both sides of the turnpike tried to stop the charging Union cavalry but to little avail.

As Confederate cavalry slowly buckled under the pressure of continued Federal assaults, Kilpatrick moved up his reserves and ordered support by artillery. The Confederate provost guard deployed on Maria Furnace Road counterattacked, trying to retake the tollgate house. Not long afterward, Iverson's North Carolina brigade, Chew's Battery, and Brig. Gen. Ambrose Wright's Georgia brigade arrived at the pass. Kilpatrick realized that he was now outnumbered. With his command scattered all along the Mason-Dixon Line, Kilpatrick ordered the remainder of his cavalry westward to Maryland. By dawn of July 5, the Union cavalry reached Ringgold and halted.

In the wake of the battle of Monterey Pass, about nine miles's worth of wagons were captured or destroyed. Upwards of 1,300 Confederate prisoners were taken, and several dozen were wounded and killed. For the Union cavalry, approximately 100 men were casualties. With the withdrawal of Kilpatrick's

This series of rocks marks the right flank of Custer's brigade during the battle of Monterey Pass. Much hand-to-hand fighting took place here. (jm)

cavalry, Monterey Pass was still in possession of the Confederate army. During that evening, the infantry corps of Hill and Longstreet bivouacked there. The last Confederate marched through on July 6.

Take a right out of the parking lot onto Route 16 (Buchanan Trail East) and travel 3.2 miles. Take a left onto Route 418 (Midvale Road) and travel for 5.6 miles. Take a left onto Ringgold Street. Immediately on your right will be a pull-off for two Civil War Trails markers.

GPS: N 39° .696223 W 77° .614741

STOP 3: LEITERSBURG

One of the biggest challenges for the retreating Confederate army was the protection of their massive wagon trains of quartermaster stores and ambulances full of wounded. Not long into the retreat, the Federal cavalry began to prey on Ewell's wagon train with quick, incessant attacks. The problem of guarding his trains grew so immense that Ewell sent several infantry brigades to bulk up the column's defense. By 5 a.m. on July 5, near Leitersburg, Maryland, Federal cavalry launched even more attacks on Ewell's massive wagon train. The 1st Vermont Cavalry attacked with speed and precision on the undefended portion of the train, capturing numerous men, wagons, and cattle.

In addition to the Confederate wagon and ambulance train, the Confederate infantry was also on the march. The Third Corps pushed on throughout July 5, passing through Fairfield before coming to rest at the foot of South Mountain. Behind the Third Corps, the First Corps also reached the South Mountain passes. The Second Corps finally received orders to get on the march on July 5. Ordered to head towards the Fairfield Road, Ewell's soldiers got moving far later than expected due to the clogged road. It took the corps nearly twelve hours to reach Fairfield, just a dozen miles southwest of Gettysburg. Nevertheless, by the late afternoon of July 5, Brig. Gen. John Brown Gordon's Georgia brigade formed the rearguard for the entire army. All elements of the Army of Northern Virginia were on the march and headed back toward the Potomac River and the safety of Virginia.

Continue on Ringgold Street for 0.5 miles and make a left onto

Leitersburg-Smithsburg Road. Travel 3.9 miles into Smithsburg and make a right onto West Water Street. After 0.3 miles, take a right into Veterans Park. Two Civil War Trails markers will be on your left along the entrance road.

GPS: N 39° .653161 W 77° .578168

STOP 4: SMITHSBURG

Elsewhere on July 5, the Union cavalry continued to probe and attack the stretched line of the Confederate retreat. Buford's division, as well as Merritt's brigade, reached Frederick, Maryland, during the day. Kilpatrick's division pushed south and deployed near Smithsburg. It had been a long road for Kilpatrick's men. Not only had they been harassing the Confederate column, but they also escorted more than 1,300 prisoners; thus, their arrival at Smithsburg around 9:00 a.m. was a welcome relief. The citizens of the town fed many men and horses while other troopers passed the time by dozing in the shade.

Even with this backdrop of relaxation, Kilpatrick was well aware of the threat of Confederate cavalry operating in the area. Accordingly, Kilpatrick ordered the defenses of three hills north, east, and south of the town itself. By the afternoon of July 5, Federals found a need for those defenses. Confederate cavalry riding with Stuart drove the Federal skirmishers in from their advanced posts. Rolling several pieces of artillery into position, Stuart then opened a bombardment on the Federal troopers and the town, striking several homes. A number of skirmishes across the front ensued throughout the remaining daylight hours before Kilpatrick broke off the action and pulled back to Boonsboro. Stuart's men quickly capitalized on the Federal withdrawal and took positions that allowed them to further guard the Confederate retreat to the Potomac River.

Turn right out of Veterans Park and travel 0.9 miles and make a right onto Route 64 (Jefferson Boulevard). Continue east on Route 64 (Jefferson Boulevard) for 6.7 miles (entering Hagerstown) and take a left onto North Cannon Avenue. After 0.1 miles, make a right onto East Franklin Avenue and then take your immediate right to stay on East Franklin Avenue. Continue on East Franklin

"Marching Prisoners to Frederick MD." (loc)

Pvt. William B. Todd of Company E, 9th Virginia Cavalry, participated in the fight at Hagerstown on July 6, 1863. (loc)

Avenue for 0.3 miles and make a left onto North Potomac Street. In about 250 feet, there will be several Civil War Trails markers on your right attached to a parking garage.

GPS: N 39° .642698 W 77° .719844

STOP 5: BATTLE OF HAGERSTOWN

Still in constant motion since the close of the battle of Gettysburg, the Union cavalry was anything but idle on July 6. Kilpatrick's division, still in Boonsboro after their withdrawal from Smithsburg, heard that Buford's division was moving towards South Mountain. Kilpatrick and Buford hurriedly met and agreed on a coordinated effort to attack the Confederate wagon trains at Williamsport and those moving through Hagerstown.

As Kilpatrick's division neared Hagerstown, his cavalry engaged with pickets of the 9th and 10th Virginia Cavalry. By noon, he pushed them aside, then ordered elements of the 18th Pennsylvania Cavalry into the town itself, where they further engaged the 9th Virginia. Soon the fight spread throughout the town, and Kilpatrick ordered more regiments into the fray. He did so in a piecemeal fashion, though, and it cost the troopers dearly. The general did not know that Confederate infantry were in Hagerstown, as well—nearly 600 infantrymen of Iverson's brigade, which poured deadly volleys into the Federal riders. Kilpatrick soon realized it was an unequal contest he could not win. Breaking off the fight, he rode with his command westward to participate with Buford on the attack against the Confederate wagon train at Williamsport.

July 6 also marked the first significant movements of the Federal army away from Gettysburg. Although the VI Corps had been following the retreating Confederate army from a safe distance, a large majority of the Federal army still remained either on the Gettysburg battlefield or in its vicinity. On this day, however, Meade received intelligence from the VI Corps that Lee's army was not stopping to make a defensive stand at South Mountain. With this news, Meade ordered the remaining Federal corps in the area around Gettysburg to concentrate at Middletown, Maryland, and use the mountain gaps, Turner's and Crampton's, to reach

Pvt. Charles Chapman of Company A, 10th Virginia Cavalry, left, with an unidentified soldier, right, also fought at Hagerstown on July 6. (loc)

This period image shows the camp of the 18th Pennsylvania Cavalry at their winter quarters at Brandy Station, December 1863-April 1864. (loc)

the Confederate army before they could cross the swollen Potomac River.

Continue on South Potomac Street and take your next left onto East Washington Street. Travel 2.4 miles and make a right onto South Edgewood Drive. Travel 1.4 miles (through Funkstown; Edgewood Drive will become Alt-40) and make a right into a parking lot. The Civil War Trails marker will be at the southern end of the parking lot facing the highway.

GPS: N 39° .600591 W 77° .703094

STOP 6: BATTLE OF FUNKSTOWN

After several days of hard marching, by July 9, the Army of the Potomac's infantry corps had not only reached their Middletown objective, but had pushed west through and beyond the mountain gaps. The army, now concentrated, would not move further until Meade had better intelligence on the exact location of the Confederate army and the strength of its position. Once again, Meade relied on the Federal cavalry to achieve this. During this mission on July 10, Federal and Confederate cavalry clashed at Funkstown. The Confederate cavalry were ready for the fight. Lee had ordered Stuart to operate in this area to continue buying time for the Army of Northern Virginia to strengthen its position while it awaited a crossing of the Potomac.

"The 6th Corps crossing the bridge at Funkstown in pursuit of Genl. Lee's forces after Gettysburg." (loc)

"July 10, attacked the enemy at 8 a.m. and drove him through Funkstown," wrote Buford in his official report of the campaign. Stuart and his troopers fought on the defensive throughout the battle, the first time they had taken a defensive posture since reentering Maryland. Fighting waged all day. Both sides added infantry support as the battle grew. Nearing 3:00 p.m., Buford's troopers were running low on—and in some instances, out of—ammunition for their carbines. "At 3 p.m. I could no longer reply with carbines, for want of cartridges, and consequently ordered the division to fall back," reported Buford. Infantry from the VI Corps arrived to the fight. Much to their surprise, they encountered not Confederate cavalry but infantry. For the first time since the battle of Gettysburg, Federal and Confederate infantry clashed again.

By nightfall, the Federal cavalry looked to flank and cut off Stuart's position. The Confederate cavalryman would not let this happen, and "by a secret movement at night, it was deemed prudent to withdraw . . . which was accordingly done," Stuart noted in his report of the affair. Of the men engaged in the battle of Funkstown, Buford noted, "There was no faltering or hesitation. Each man went to work determined to carry anything in reason." Stuart was also happy with how his men performed. They had fought in battle "with great skill and effect," while the infantry that fought alongside them had "participated very creditably, indeed. . . ."

Turn right out of the parking lot onto Alternate Route 40 east and travel 5.6 miles. Turn right into the parking lot, and the Civil War Trails marker is near the parking lot entrance.

GPS: N 39° .526340 W 77° .663859

STOP 7: BATTLE OF BOONSBORO

The engagement at Funkstown on July 10 was not the first time Confederate cavalry had tangled with their Federal counterpart in order to allow the Army of Northern Virginia more time to strengthen its position at Williamsport. Two days earlier, on July 8, the largest cavalry battle during the Confederate retreat occurred at Boonsboro, Maryland. Along the National and Williamsport Roads in Boonsboro, Stuart organized a major assault against Buford's and Kilpatrick's Federal cavalry to buy that time. Stuart reported that he ordered the attack "in order, by a bold demonstration, to threaten an advance upon the enemy." The cavalry clash was anything but traditional. The recent rains had turned the fields and roads into a quagmire, so charges were all but out of the question. In many cases, such as with Jones's brigade, the assaults were made dismounted. As "the animated fight" continued, however, Union infantry arrived to support the Federal troopers. Stuart's riders, low on ammunition and suffering from exhaustion—both the men and their mounts—were not be able to sustain an attack from such heavy numbers, so the general called off the fight. Buford and Kilpatrick pulled back, as well. Stuart believed he accomplished his goal—"The move was successful," he wrote—and he ordered his command to Funkstown to the north.

Turn right out of the parking lot onto Alternate Route 40 east and travel 0.5 miles. Turn right onto Route 68 (Lappans Road). Travel 3.3 miles and make a right into the parking lot (just after you cross Antietam Creek). The Civil War Trails marker will be on the edge of the parking lot. After reading the marker, we encourage you to explore the area and visit Booth's Mill Bridge.

GPS: N 39° .538604 W 77° .710454

STOP 8: BOOTH'S MILL BRIDGE: MEADE'S COUNCIL OF WAR

By July 11, the Army of the Potomac's aggressive pursuit of Lee's retreating army had slowed drastically. The Union soldiers had endured hard marching since July 6, and Meade, not knowing

A drawing by James Kelly depicts the July 2, 1863, council of war Meade held at his headquarters during the battle. Although different officers were present during his second and third councils of war, due to wounds that some of his officer corps received in combat at Gettysburg, a much similar scene would have presented itself at Meade's headquarters at the end of the Gettysburg campaign. (loc)

when another battle might take place, needed his army in a condition to fight. Thus, all of the Federal infantry corps remained in their positions at a safe distance opposite of the Confederate line around Williamsport on July 11. The Union cavalry remained mostly inactive, as well, with only small probes and repositioning during the day. Opposite of the Federal inactivity, the Army of Northern Virginia continued to strengthen their entrenched position. By the hour, it became stronger and more formidable. General Lee wrote of the day, "nothing but occasional skirmishing occurred. . . ."

Twenty-four hours later, the situation changed. On July 12, as the heavy fog of the early morning lifted, Buford, armed with startling intelligence, wired his commanding officer, General Pleasonton. Buford told Pleasonton that most of the Confederate army was not crossing the Potomac, and those who were—the sick and wounded—had to be ferried by one flat boat. This report, coupled with dozens of others that flooded into Meade's headquarters throughout the early portion of the day, left him with the picture that Lee's army was pinned against a flooded Potomac with nowhere to go. The rest of the day continued to support this notion as severe skirmishing between the two lines of battle gleaned further intelligence. At the same time, the Federal line became solidified as the I, VI, and XI Corps marched north and west beyond Funkstown, producing a continuous line of battle for the army—from Hagerstown on the right to Sharpsburg on the left.

Meade, with his army in position and strengthening, wrote Halleck in Washington at 4:30 p.m.: "It is my intention to attack them to-morrow, [July 13] unless something intervenes to prevent it, for the reason that delay will strengthen the enemy and will not increase my force."

Just hours later, something intervened. Meade called together at his headquarters that evening a council of war, the third during the campaign. The commanding general sought advice from his senior-ranking officers as to whether they should attack the strong position of the Confederate army or not, knowing that the Confederates were pinned against the Potomac. As Meade wired Halleck the following afternoon, "five out of six (of my corps commanders) were unqualifiedly opposed to it. . . . Under these circumstances . . . I did not feel myself authorized to attack until I had made more careful examination of the enemy's position, strength, and defensive works."

Halleck, the War Department, and President Lincoln were aghast. Late in the evening on July 13, Halleck wired Meade: "You are strong enough to attack and defeat the enemy before he can effect a crossing. Act upon your own judgment and make your generals execute your orders. Call no council of war. It is proverbial that councils of war never fight."

Turn right out of the parking lot onto Route 68 (Lappans Road) and travel 1.8 miles. Make a left onto Route 65 (Sharpsburg Pike) and then take an immediate right into the gas station. The Civil War Trails sign will be on your left as you enter the gas station.

GPS: N 39° .553142 W 77° .737605

STOP 9: JONES'S CROSSROADS

Before Meade's council of war on July 12, two days earlier, on July 10, Meade worked to secure the right flank of his army near Funkstown. This was just one reason that battle had erupted there that day. Those units not involved in that process, the army's left flank, marched throughout July 10 to reach a concentration point near Jones's Crossroads.

A farmer from New York before the war, Col. Charles Wainwright's work as the I Corps artillery commander and their defense of Cemetery Hill during the battle of Gettysburg was critical for the Union army's line of battle. His insightful wartime diary, later published, remains one of the best diaries from an officer in the Union army. (gnmp)

The II, III, and XII Corps, as well as the army's reserve artillery train, not only arrived at Jones's Crossroads during July 10, but also made a strong anchor for the Federal left flank. As this portion of the army worked to strengthen this position, only miles from the Confederate line, Col. Charles Wainwright, commander of the I Corps artillery, commented on those living in the area. "There is a difference between the people of Maryland and those of Pennsylvania:

A man of some fifty or more stood looking at our men pull down the fences to start their breastworks. . . . Having a fellow-feeling for the owner as a brother farmer, I spoke to the man and said it was hard on the owner of the land to destroy his crops and fences so. 'Oh,' says he, 'you may destroy my whole farm if you will only whip the rebels.' If the eastern Marylanders are the most bitter of the rebels, those west of Frederick are the truest Union people I have met with anywhere."

Exit the parking lot on the other side of the gas station and make a left onto Route 68 (Lappans Road). Travel 4.3 miles and make a left into the Williamsport Red Men Lodge. Follow the entrance road until you get to the parking lot. The Civil War Trails marker will be on your right.

GPS: N 39° .579398 W 77° .808218

STOP 10: THE WAGONER'S FIGHT

The Army of Northern Virginia's position at Williamsport was incredibly strong after the army had worked days to dig in. That was not the case when the first elements of Lee's army reached the Potomac River crossing here just days after the battle of Gettysburg had ended. At five o'clock on the afternoon of July 6, the massive wagon train of supplies and ambulances heavily laden with the wounded of Lee's army at Williamsport came under attack. Buford's division of 3,500 horsemen and eighteen cannon, which had left Frederick more than twelve hours earlier, reached the Confederate train's concentration and crossing point. Buford arrived with plenty of daylight left in order to organize and deliver a catastrophic attack, especially with the arrival of Kilpatrick's division on Buford's right.

Imboden at Williamsport knew he needed reinforcements and fast. Although Lee pushed his leading infantry units hard to arrive at Williamsport to strengthen the defense of the wagon train, the Union assault began before they arrived. Thus, to add weight to his numbers, Imboden pressed into service approximately 700 wagoners and walking wounded, distributing rifles to them and placing them on the front line. Helping to command these men were numerous Confederate officers who were wounded at Gettysburg and were part of the train, including Col. John M. Stone of the 2nd Mississippi and Maj. Alfred Belo of the 55th North Carolina. In all, Imboden was able to assemble a force of about 2,500 men from various elements of the army. The extra "reinforcements" worked, not only repelling the Union thrust, but also driving some of Kilpatrick's men from the field in an astonishing counterattack.

The wagoners defended the train at Williamsport successfully; no wagons were lost. More battle-hardened veterans of the Confederate infantry and cavalry arrived at darkness to shore up the line. Buford's division, with nearing darkness, pulled back towards the relative safety of Boonsboro.

Native North Carolinian Maj. Alfred Belo, served in the 55th North Carolina Infantry and was wounded during the battle of Gettysburg. Belo was fortunate and was evacuated from Gettysburg during the army's retreat; despite his wound, however, he was pressed into service to help defend the wagon train at Williamsport. (wc)

Return to Route 68 (Lappans Road) and make a left. Travel 0.4 miles and make a left onto Route 63 (Spielman Road). In 0.9 miles, make a right onto Falling Waters Road. In 2.9 miles, the road will go up a ridge. On your right will be the Donnelly House and the location of the mortal wounding of Brig. Gen. James Pettigrew. The house and grounds are private property, so please do not trespass. The ridge is the general area of the Confederate line in this area. It was not until the twenty-first century that a group formed to promote preservation of the battlefield here. Continue down Falling Waters Road and it will dead end at the Potomac Fish and Game Club. Turn around and the tour will begin back at the Donnelly House location.

GPS: N 39° .552940 W 77° .852998

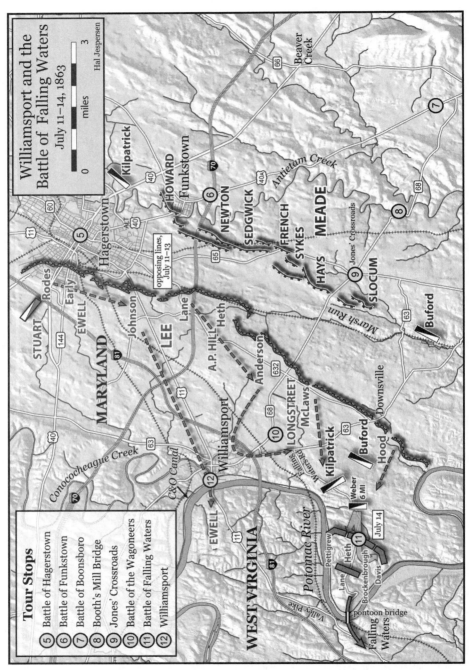

Williamsport and the Battle of Falling Waters
July 11–14, 1863
Hal Jespersen

miles
0   3

Tour Stops

(5) Battle of Hagerstown
(6) Battle of Funkstown
(7) Battle of Boonsboro
(8) Booth's Mill Bridge
(9) Jones' Crossroads
(10) Battle of the Wagoneers
(11) Battle of Falling Waters
(12) Williamsport

WILLAMSPORT AND THE BATTLE OF FALLING WATERS—The Confederate retreat from Gettysburg was marked by numerous cavalry actions between Union and Confederate cavalry. Several times these engagements were augmented by infantry supports. Now, in the final days of the campaign, Robert E. Lee waited to get his army back across the Potomac River.

A modern image of the Donnelly House, part of the Confederate defensive position at Falling Waters in July 1863. Fighting swirled around the house and barn, no longer standing, and also witnessed the mortal wounding of James J. Pettigrew. (dw)

STOP 11: BATTLE OF FALLING WATERS: DONNELLY HOUSE

In the early hours of July 14, 1863, Federal cavalry under the command of Kilpatrick pushed aggressively forward towards the Confederate line. He and his troopers were heading towards the river crossing at Williamsport. Along the way, they captured numerous Confederate pickets and stragglers. As they neared Williamsport, Kilpatrick learned that a significant portion of the Confederate army still waited to cross the Potomac at Falling Waters, so he quickly changed the direction of his advancing column to head there. Kilpatrick's intelligence was accurate. Elements of the Third Corps, after being on the march for more than twelve hours, still waited on the north bank of the river.

A little later that

The battlefield at Falling Waters, site of the Confederate works and the charge of the Federal cavalry. (dw)

"Charge of the 6th Michigan cavalry over the rebel earthworks nr. Falling Waters" by Alfred Waud. The sketch depicts the moment when the 6th Michigan slammed into the Rebel earthworks on the Donnelly property. (loc)

morning, around 7:00 a.m., Buford's troopers began an aggressive push to test the strength of the Confederate defenses. Within thirty minutes, Buford realized those entrenchments were empty. Buford's and Kilpatrick's commands soon engaged the last remnants of Lee's army yet to cross at Falling Waters. These men, of Henry Heth's division, witnessed cavalry approaching their position, but assumed it was Stuart and his troopers; Heth's men continued at ease in camp with rifles stacked. Kilpatrick pounced on the unsuspecting Rebels, ordering the 6th Michigan Cavalry to charge. The scene was pandemonium. Hand-to-hand combat broke out along the line. Numerous men were killed and wounded, including Maj. Peter Weber of the Michigan regiment, dead on the field, and Confederate Gen. Pettigrew, mortally wounded. Hundreds of Confederate soldiers were captured even as more Confederate infantry rushed to the fight to beat back the continuous Federal attacks.

Close to real-time intelligence flooded into Meade's headquarters. Although a majority of Lee's

A different view of the battle of Falling Waters, titled **"Gallant charge by two companies of the 6th Michigan on Tuesday morning on the rebel rearguard, near Falling Waters, where part of the rebel army crossed the Potomac."** Sketched by Edwin Forbes on July 14, 1863, it shows the Donnelly house, barn, and retreat of Confederate infantry from their works under the weight of the cavalry attack. (loc)

army had already escaped over the Potomac, Meade ordered his men to push towards Williamsport and the Potomac. The I, V, VI, and XI Corps, as well as a division of the XII, maneuvered in that direction while the II and III Corps raced to Falling Waters. Buford, already there, saw the Confederate pontoon bridge and ordered his troopers forward to capture it. "The enemy's bridge was protected by over a dozen guns in position and sharpshooters on the Virginia side," reported Buford, and "As our troops neared the bridge, the enemy cut the Maryland side loose, and the bridge swung to the Virginia side."

Lee's army made it back to the safety of Virginia.

Retrace your route 2.8 miles and make a left onto Route 63 (Spielman Road). In 1.6 miles, make a left onto Route 68 (Lappans Road). Travel 3.7 miles (entering into Williamsport) and make a left onto Frederick Street. Then in one block, make a right onto Vermont Street. Follow Vermont Street for three blocks and make a left onto Potomac Street. In one block, the entrance for the C&O Canal National Historical Park will be on your right. The Civil War Trails marker is on the C&O Canal towpath facing the river. If you are interested, you can walk the towpath east and there are interpretive markers related to the Confederate crossing points. These are 2-3 miles down the towpath.

GPS: N 39° .600843 W 77° .827613

STOP 12: WILLIAMSPORT

The crossing of the last units of the Confederate army at Falling Waters took place on the morning of July 14. However, Lee began crossing other units of the army upriver at Williamsport hours earlier, on the evening of July 13.

Although the Federal cavalry reconnoitered, and the infantry constructed some entrenchments, July 13 passed by quietly for the Army of the Potomac across from Williamsport. Quiet, too, was the scene along the strong position of the Army of Northern Virginia.

An Alfred Waud period sketch of Williamsport, Maryland. The surrounding landscape transformed as the Confederate army dug in and prepared for a possible Union assault. (loc)

Williamsport and the Potomac River crossing. (dw)

By early evening, however, that was about to change. The water levels of the Potomac had receded enough for the men to make it to the far side, so Lee ordered the crossing of the Potomac at Williamsport to begin.

Crossing at Williamsport was Gen. Ewell's Second Corps. His men reached the site just as darkness fell. Rodes's division, the first to leave the defensive position and make for the crossing, was quickly attacked during the process. Rodes's men made short work of the Federal attempt and moved on to the Potomac. Next in line was Early's division, which was followed by Johnson's, the last in Ewell's corps. When Ewell himself arrived at the crossing, he found nothing but chaos: "I could find no ferry-boats, nor any one in charge; it was dark and raining. Everything was in confusion." Ewell quickly took charge and ordered his artillery and

Alfred Waud's sketch, "On the Potomac nr. Williamsport. Rebel crossing; Rebel Pontoons at Falling Waters," captures the moments when Ewell's Second Corps crossed the river back to the safety of Virginia. (loc)

The full view of the Cumberland Valley from High Rock. (dw)

wagon trains to utilize the nearby pontoon, recently completed. He sent the rest of his corps to the river crossing. "Just before midnight, my advance commenced crossing," he wrote. "The men had directions to sling their cartridge-boxes over their shoulders, but many rounds of ammunition were necessarily lost, as the water was up to their armpits the whole way across, sometimes deeper."

By 8:00 a.m. on July 14, Early's division reached the Virginia side of the Potomac River and safety. Not long after, Stuart's column, bringing up the rear of the column, crossed here, as well. At Falling Waters downriver, the final elements of the Army of Northern Virginia would finish their crossing of the Potomac River later that morning.

The Gettysburg campaign was over.

EPILOGUE

The Gettysburg campaign was over. On July 14, 1863, General Halleck in Washington received a telegram from Meade informing him: "I found, on reaching his [Confederate] lines, that they were evacuated." Seeking input from Halleck in the same telegram, "Your instructions as to further movements . . . are desired." Within the hour a shocked Halleck responded. "The enemy should be pursued and cut up." Halleck also revealed that Lincoln, who had assumed the latest commanding officer of the Army of Potomac understood the necessity of destroying Lee's army, not just pushing it out of the Pennsylvania, was crestfallen. "I need hardly say to you that the escape of Lee's army without another battle has created great dissatisfaction in the mind of the President, and it will require an active and energetic pursuit on your part to remove the impression that it has not been sufficiently active heretofore."

When Meade read Halleck's words, he took Lincoln's "dissatisfaction" as a censure, wiring back his resignation. Meanwhile, Lincoln sat down at the White House to further express his dissatisfaction with Meade in a letter to the Army of the Potomac's commanding general. "The case, summarily stated is this . . . you stood and let the flood run down, bridges be built, and the enemy move away at his leisure, without attacking him," seethed Lincoln. Furthermore, "I do not believe you appreciate the magnitude of the misfortune involved in

Following battle at Gettysburg, the two armies remained in almost constant contact through the rest of the summer and fall of 1863. (cm)

One can almost see the sigh on Lincoln's shoulders, exasperated by Meade's inability to follow up the victory at Gettysburg with a more complete victory in the days that followed. (loc)

Lee's escape. He was within your easy grasp, and to have closed upon him would, in connection with our other late successes, have ended the war."

When the president completed his letter to Meade, he ultimately let cooler heads prevail. After waiting several days to send the emotional letter, Lincoln shelved it permanently. On the envelope was written "never sent, unsigned." Lincoln ultimately stood by Meade, and the commanding general retained his command of the Army of the Potomac.

Lincoln, Halleck, the War Department, and northern citizens were not the only ones upset by Lee's escape back into Virginia. Many men in the Army of the Potomac immediately recognized the significance of the Rebel army's escape. Ambrose Thompson, 5th Connecticut Volunteer Infantry, wrote home on July 18, "I think we are completely outgeneraled and nothing to say in our favor. Lee went into Penn. wasted, destroyed, and carried off all he could for 3 weeks and now is back in Va again, without our forces even once attacking him but merely acting on the defensive all the time. Even allowing he has suffered the greatest loss, it is a burning shame to think he is back again at all."

Despite Meade's detractors, he had accomplished much since taking command of the Army of the Potomac on June 28. He increased the pace of his marching columns, brought his army to battle, and bested Lee and his Army of Northern Virginia. Although many thought the pace of his pursuit lacked the same vigor as when the army had moved north through Maryland and Pennsylvania, Meade faced numerous obstacles to bring Lee to battle once more.

First, the Army of the Potomac had suffered for more than a month from the grueling campaign as well as from weather conditions. Frederick Connette, an infantryman in the 14th United States Infantry, spoke to this point when he wrote to a friend on July 17: "I hope they will give a sufficient rest and clothing to the Army or it would be demoralized and spoiled forever. . . ." An active and vigorous pursuit by an army in this condition would have been next to impossible. Meade's army had also experienced grievous casualties at Gettysburg:

approximately 23,000 men killed, wounded, missing, or captured.

Second, the Army of the Potomac faced a military conundrum during their pursuit. While the Confederate army fell back to their extended lines, it added men into the ranks and grew stronger. Meade in pursuit, however, stretched his communication and supply lines, and he decreased his fighting forces to protect those lines. The Army of Northern Virginia was wounded and caged for the moment by the swollen Potomac River, but Lee's army still had plenty of fight left in it.

As Lee and the Army of Northern Virginia moved deeper into the safety of the state of Virginia, the commanding general, Confeder-

A monument commemorating the burning of Chambersburg sits in the town square opposite the courthouse. (cm)

ate president, and Southern populace had an opportunity to reflect and take stock of the recent campaign. Assessing the results against Lee's stated objectives—approved in May 1863 by Davis— the Army of Northern Virginia had been mostly successful. Lee had driven the Union army from Virginia during the six weeks' campaign, a stated objective. He had also driven Union forces from the Shenandoah Valley, another goal of the advance northward. Yet, in the weeks following the campaign, as the Union army returned to familiar ground in Virginia, many began to wonder whether these objectives could be claimed as a success after all.

If viewed as a raid, the Confederate army amassed an immense amount of supplies during their time in Maryland and Pennsylvania. Vital food, fodder, and medical supplies filled a steady stream of wagon trains to the rear as Lee's army moved northward. Although he lived off the land and then some—another campaign objective—he was unable to relieve the Virginia farmers long enough to plant and harvest a new crop.

Lee's objective of bringing the Federal army to battle on northern soil was likewise limited in its success. Although he had indeed brought the Army of the Potomac to battle on Pennsylvania soil, the outcome was not the stunning victory he had hoped for. The lost battle gave Lee even less hope that the northern peace movement would help the Confederate cause.

Although the campaign and battle at Gettysburg ended with mixed results—viewed through the lens of Lee's campaign objectives—there is no denying the effect the battle had on his army. The Confederate army sustained approximately 28,000 casualties, killed, wounded, missing, or captured— a number the army nor the Confederacy could afford to lose. Among the dead were numerous experienced officers who would be nearly impossible to replace. Generals Hood, Pettigrew, Pender, and many lower-level officers had all been lost. Despite the losses, though, the morale in Lee's army remained high.

Lee's own morale, however, sank in the weeks following the Gettysburg campaign. The general took the loss seriously and personally. As the Southern press and some in the Confederate Congress began to question the success of the campaign and its cost, Lee, at his headquarters in Orange Court House, tendered his resignation to Davis: "I have been prompted by these reflections more than once since my return from Pennsylvania to propose to Your Excellency the propriety of selecting another commander for this army," Lee wrote August 8.

He also fretted over public opinion and the reaction of his men and officers: "I have seen and

While the Gettysburg campaign represented the last road north for Robert E. Lee's Army of Northern Virginia, Confederate raiders swept into Chambersburg, Pennsylvania, in July 1864. After their demands for ransom were denied, Confederates burned the town, as depicted in *Harper's Weekly.* (hw)

heard of expression of discontent in the public journals at the result of the expedition." Lee cited his poor physical health, an issue throughout the most recent campaign, as a reason to be relieved. "Everything, therefore, points to the advantages to be derived from a new commander, and I the more anxiously urge the matter upon Your Excellency from my belief that a younger and abler man than myself can readily be attained." Like Lincoln with Meade, Davis did not accept the resignation, and Lee remained the commander of the Army of Northern Virginia for the remainder of the war.

Of the 165,000 men engaged, more than 51,000 ended up as casualties. More than 3,500 of those Union soldiers were interred here in Gettysburg National Cemetery. (cm)

With the strategic Federal victories at Vicksburg and the success of the Tullahoma campaign, the summer of 1863 became a turning point in the war. Additionally, the Gettysburg campaign proved that the vaunted Army of Northern Virginia and its famed commander could be beaten on the field of battle. The turning point, however, did not mean the end of the war nor the end of Lee's offensive plans, as he demonstrated again that fall during the Bristoe Station campaign. The war, meanwhile, would carry on for almost two more long and bloody years.

Suggested Reading

Out Flew the Sabers: The Battle of Brandy Station, June 9, 1863
by Eric Wittenberg and Daniel T. Davis
(Savas Beatie, 2016)
ISBN-13: 978-1-61121-256-3

Fight Like the Devil: The First Day at Gettysburg, July 1, 1863
by Chris Mackowski, Kristopher D. White, and
Daniel T. Davis
(Savas Beatie, 2015)
ISBN-13: 978-1-61121-227-3

Don't Give an Inch: The Second Day at Gettysburg, July 2, 1863—From Little Round Top to Cemetery Ridge
by Chris Mackowski, Kristopher D. White, and
Daniel T. Davis
(Savas Beatie, 2016)
ISBN-13: 978-1-61121-229-7

Stay and Fight It Out: The Second Day at Gettysburg, July 2, 1863—Culp's Hill and the North End of the Battlefield
by Chris Mackowski, Kristopher D. White, and
Daniel T. Davis
(Savas Beatie, 2017)
ISBN-13: 978-1-61121-331-7

We Gained Nothing but Glory: The Third Day at Gettysburg, July 3, 1863
by Chris Mackowski, Kristopher D. White, and
Daniel T. Davis
(Savas Beatie, 2017)
ISBN-13: 978-1-61121-231-0

BOOKS BEYOND EMERGING CIVIL WAR

Retreat from Gettysburg: Lee, Logistics, and the Pennsylvania Campaign
by Kent Masterson Brown
(The University of North Carolina Press, 2011)
ISBN-13: 978-0-80787-209-3

The Gettysburg Campaign: A Study in Command
by Edwin Coddington
(Touchstone, 1997)
ISBN-13: 978-0-68484-569-2

The Maps of Gettysburg: An Atlas of the Gettysburg Campaign, June 3 – July 13, 1863
by Bradley Gottfried
(Savas Beatie, 2010)
ISBN-13: 978-1-93271-482-1

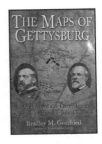

Confrontation at Gettysburg: A Nation Saved, A Cause Lost
by John Hoptak
(The History Press, 2012)
ISBN-13: 978-1-60949-426-1

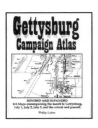

*Gettysburg Campaign Atlas: Revised and Expanded, 444
Maps Encompassing the March to Gettysburg, July 1, July 2,
July 3, and the Retreat and Pursuit*
by Philip Laino
(Gettysburg Publishing LLC, 2015)
ISBN-13: 978-0-98386-314-4

*The Cavalry Battles of Aldie, Middleburg and Upperville:
June 10-27, 1863*
by Robert O'Neill
(H.E. Howard, 1993)
ISBN-13: 978-1-56190-052-7

Gettysburg
by Stephen Sears
(Mariner Books, 2004)
ISBN-13: 978-0-61848-538-3

Gettysburg: A Testing of Courage
by Noah Trudreau
(Harper Perennial, 2003)
ISBN-13: 978-0-06093-186-5

*The Confederate Approach on Harrisburg:: The Gettysburg
Campaign's Northernmost Reaches*
by Cooper H. Wingert
(The History Press, 2012)
ISBN-13: 978-1-60949-858-0

*The Second Battle of Winchester: The Confederate Victory
that Opened the Door to Gettysburg*
by Eric Wittenberg and Scott L. Mingus, Sr.
(Savas Beatie, 2015)
ISBN-13: 978-1-61121-288-4

About the Authors

Rob Orrison has worked in the history field for more than 20 years. Born and raised in Loudoun County, Virginia, Rob received his BA in Historic Preservation at Longwood College (now University) and received his MA in Public History from George Mason University. Rob currently serves as the historic site operations supervisor for Prince William County. Outside of work, Rob leads tours with Civil War Excursion Tours (which he co-founded), and he contributes to the Emerging Civil War blog. Rob serves as treasurer of the Historic House Museum Consortium of Washington, DC, and serves on the board of directors for the Bull Run Civil War Roundtable, the Mosby Heritage Area Association, Virginia Civil War Trails, and the Governing Council of the Virginia Association of Museums. In 2015, he co-authored *A Want of Vigilance: The Bristoe Station Campaign.* He lives in Prince William County with his wife, Jamie, and son, Carter.

Dan Welch received his BA in Instrumental Music Education from Youngstown State University and his MA in Military History with a Civil War-Era concentration at American Military University. Welch currently serves as a primary and secondary educator with a public school district in northeast Ohio. Previously, Dan was the education programs coordinator for the Gettysburg Foundation, the non-profit partner of Gettysburg National Military Park. Dan continues to serve as a seasonal Park Ranger at Gettysburg National Military Park in the Interpretation Division, where he has worked since 2009. During that time, he has led numerous programs on the campaign and the battle for school groups, families, and visitors of all ages. He is also a contributor to the Emerging Civil War blog. He currently resides with his wife, Sarah, in Boardman, Ohio.

EMERGING CIVIL WAR SERIES